FreePBX 2.5
Powerful Telephony Solutions

Configure, deploy, and maintain an enterprise-class
VoIP PBX

Alex Robar

PUBLISHING

BIRMINGHAM - MUMBAI

FreePBX 2.5 Powerful Telephony Solutions

First published: August 2009

Production Reference: 1200809

Published by Packt Publishing Ltd.
32 Lincoln Road
Olton
Birmingham, B27 6PA, UK.

ISBN 978-1-847194-72-5

www.packtpub.com

Cover Image by Vinayak Chittar (vinayak.chittar@gmail.com)

Credits

Author
Alex Robar

Reviewer
Justin Zimmer

Acquisition Editor
Sarah Cullington

Development Editor
Darshana D. Shinde

Technical Editors
Conrad Sardinha

Charumathi Sankaran

Copy Editor
Sanchari Mukherjee

Indexer
Rekha Nair

Editorial Team Leader
Gagandeep Singh

Project Team Leader
Priya Mukherji

Project Coordinator
Leena Purkait

Proofreader
Lynda Sliwoski

Drawing Coordinator
Nilesh Mohite

Production Coordinator
Shantanu Zagade

Cover Work
Shantanu Zagade

About the Author

Alex Robar is a strong supporter of Open Source Software and has worked in the IT industry for seven years. He has worked with Digium's Asterisk software since version 1.2, and typically uses Asterisk to replace existing closed source PBX systems for SMBs. As the Technical Services Manager for GearyTech (a Canadian Managed Services Provider), he develops IT automation solutions for SMBs. He has worked with open source telephony solutions for the past four years, and has collaborated on the development and growth of an international Asterisk-based VoIP peering network.

In 2005, Alex co-authored *Secure Your E-mail Server on IBM eServer i5 with Linux*, an IBM Redpaper on using OSS solutions on the iSeries server platform to create an integrated security appliance for a small business. Alex has also authored several freely available short tutorials for Asterisk and FreePBX.

I would like to thank my parents for always supporting my inner geek, no matter what, my sister Amanda for always giving me her time even when I was unable to give her mine, and my fiancée Eveline who has always pushed her own interests aside to help support mine when I needed it.

I would also like to thank Leena Purkait and Darshana Shinde of Packt Publishing for keeping me on track throughout this entire process, and helping me solve whatever difficulties I had.

About the Reviewer

Justin Zimmer has worked in the contact center technology field for over ten years. During that time he has performed extensive software and computer telephony integrations using both PSTN and IP telephony. His current projects include system designs utilizing open source soft switches over more traditional proprietary hardware based telephony, and the integration of these technologies into market specific CRM products.

As CTO of Unicore Technologies out of Phoenix, AZ, Justin is developing hosted contact center solutions for the low-end market. Unicore's solutions present contact centers with low startup costs in a turbulent economy, and allows those centers to scale their business while maintaining a consistent and familiar user interface.

Justin has worked on countless software user manuals and instructional guides for both internal and customer usage.

He also worked on the Hopewell Blogs: a science fiction adventure novel that will be released chapter by chapter online and available in print once the final chapter has been released.

I'd like to thank the countless community contributors that have provided enough online documentation to make this book as accurate and helpful as possible. And I'd like to thank my wife Nicole for putting up with the extra hours spent reviewing this book, as well as my boys Micah and Caden and my daughter Keira for giving up some of their daddy-time for this project.

Table of Contents

Preface

FreePBX 2.5 Powerful Telephony Solutions was written to help system administrators build, configure, and maintain an enterprise class PBX using the Asterisk and FreePBX open source software packages. This book covers the complete process of going from a bare metal server to a completely configured PBX with extensions, voicemail, least cost routing, digital receptionists, and dozens of other features.

Each chapter of the book discusses a specific feature set of FreePBX. The chapters contain step-by-step set up instructions for configuring each feature alongside screenshots of the FreePBX interface. Chapters that cover the installation of Asterisk and FreePBX as well as securing the PBX once it is built, are also included.

What this book covers

In Chapter 1: *Installing FreePBX*, we discuss the base requirements for a Linux operating system that will run Asterisk and FreePBX. We step through configuring Apache and MySQL, and then proceed to download and install Asterisk and FreePBX under both CentOS and Ubuntu.

In Chapter 2: *Module Maintenance*, we introduce the modularized structure of FreePBX and the online FreePBX module repository. Instructions for installing, updating, and removing modules are provided.

In Chapter 3: *Devices and Extensions*, we cover the concept of extensions within FreePBX. We discuss both the operational modes for extensions, as well as the various types of endpoints that FreePBX makes available. Instructions are provided for configuring extensions, users and devices, as well as voicemail boxes.

In Chapter 4: *Trunks*, we introduce the concept of trunking as a method of connecting our PBX to the outside world. Instructions are provided for setting up each type of trunk that FreePBX supports. We also discuss methods for checking the status of configured trunks to make sure that nothing has failed.

In Chapter 5: *Basic Call Targets*, we explain the concept of directing inbound calls to call targets. Usage instructions are provided for sending calls to a termination target, an extension, or a voicemail box. Step-by-step instructions are provided for configuring ring groups, conferences, day night modes, and phonebook directories.

In Chapter 6: *Advanced Call Targets*, we provide step-by-step instructions for configuring queues, time conditions, time groups, and IVRs (digital receptionists).

In Chapter 7: *Call Routing*, we discuss directing inbound calls to the call targets created in Chapters 5 and 6. We also discuss routing outbound calls over specific trunks, and setting up outbound routes to achieve least cost routing.

In Chapter 8: *Recording Calls*, we delve into the call recording features of FreePBX. Instructions are provided for setting up permanent or selective call recording for specific extensions, conferences, or queues.

In Chapter 9: *Personalizing Your PBX*, we introduce some FreePBX features that allow us to make our PBX on our own. Step-by-step instructions are provided for configuring custom music on hold, voice prompts, feature codes, applications, and destinations. We discuss how to set up FreePBX to call back inbound callers and how to provide dial tone to external callers who are not calling from an extension on the PBX. We also cover how to configure FreePBX to check additional sources for caller ID information if none is provided, and how to configure PIN sets to password protect various FreePBX features.

In Chapter 10: *System Protection, Backup and Restoration*, we cover the concept of ensuring that our PBX is protected against failure. We discuss backing and restoring our FreePBX configuration data in case our PBX does encounter a failure.

In Chapter 11: *Security and Access Control*, we provide steps that should be taken to secure our PBX against malicious users and unauthorized access. Instructions for updating the operating system, updating Asterisk, securing MySQL, securing remote access, and configuring FreePBX administrator accounts are provided.

In Appendix A: *FreePBX Modules*, we provide a listing of all modules available for installation from the online repository and their functions.

In Appendix B: *Feature Codes*, we list all of the default feature codes and their actions.

In Appendix C: *Voicemail.conf Options*, we provide options that affect the behavior of a mailbox and the way the voicemail messages are received and processed.

In Appendix D: *Common Trunk Configurations*, we provide the trunk configuration settings for common VoIP providers.

What you need for this book

This book assumes a basic knowledge of Linux and telephony, though neither is strictly required. All commands that need to be run are provided and concepts that need to be understood are explained.

This book requires a server that is capable of running Linux, Asterisk, and FreePBX. The hardware requirements for the server will depend upon how many calls the PBX will be routing, and which actions callers can perform once they reach the PBX (for example, a PBX that records every call will require more resources than one that does not). The server should not have any operating system on it to start with. Recommended installation options are provided for both CentOS and Ubuntu.

Who this book is for

This book is written for systems administrators who want to get started with Asterisk and FreePBX. This book is perfect for administrators who want to reduce costs by replacing a proprietary PBX with a PBX that runs on open source packages, or an administrator who needs their PBX to do more than it currently does. Anyone who wants to build a stable, feature rich PBX will find this book useful.

Conventions

In this book, you will find a number of styles of text that distinguish between different kinds of information. Here are some examples of these styles, and an explanation of their meaning.

Code words in text are shown as follows: "Replace newpassword with the password you would like to set for the MySQL root user."

A block of code is set as follows:

```
#!/bin/bash

# Change this path to reflect your backup storage
# location (default is /var/lib/asterisk/backups)
BACKUPS=/var/lib/asterisk/backups
```

Any command-line input or output is written as follows:

```
sed -i "s/Port 22/Port 38000/" /etc/ssh/sshd_config
/etc/init.d/ssh restart
```

New terms and **important words** are shown in bold. Words that you see on the screen, in menus or dialog boxes for example, appear in the text like this: "In order to set up a backup, click on the **Tools** tab at the top of the navigation menu on the left".

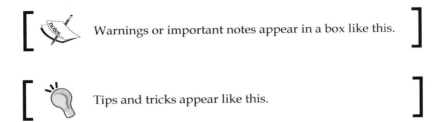

[Warnings or important notes appear in a box like this.]

[Tips and tricks appear like this.]

Reader feedback

Feedback from our readers is always welcome. Let us know what you think about this book—what you liked or may have disliked. Reader feedback is important for us to develop titles that you really get the most out of.

To send us general feedback, simply send an email to feedback@packtpub.com, and mention the book title via the subject of your message.

If there is a book that you need and would like to see us publish, please send us a note in the **SUGGEST A TITLE** form on www.packtpub.com or email suggest@packtpub.com.

If there is a topic that you have expertise in and you are interested in either writing or contributing to a book on, see our author guide on www.packtpub.com/authors.

Customer support

Now that you are the proud owner of a Packt book, we have a number of things to help you to get the most from your purchase.

Downloading the example code for the book

Visit http://www.packtpub.com/files/code/4725_Code.zip to directly download the example code.

The downloadable files contain instructions on how to use them.

Errata

Although we have taken every care to ensure the accuracy of our content, mistakes do happen. If you find a mistake in one of our books—maybe a mistake in the text or the code—we would be grateful if you would report this to us. By doing so, you can save other readers from frustration, and help us to improve subsequent versions of this book. If you find any errata, please report them by visiting http://www.packtpub.com/support, selecting your book, clicking on the **let us know** link, and entering the details of your errata. Once your errata are verified, your submission will be accepted and the errata added to any list of existing errata. Any existing errata can be viewed by selecting your title from http://www.packtpub.com/support.

Piracy

Piracy of copyright material on the Internet is an ongoing problem across all media. At Packt, we take the protection of our copyright and licenses very seriously. If you come across any illegal copies of our works, in any form, on the Internet, please provide us with the location address or web site name immediately so that we can pursue a remedy.

Please contact us at copyright@packtpub.com with a link to the suspected pirated material.

We appreciate your help in protecting our authors, and our ability to bring you valuable content.

Questions

You can contact us at questions@packtpub.com if you are having a problem with any aspect of the book, and we will do our best to address it.

1
Installing FreePBX

FreePBX is a dynamic software package that uses the power of Linux, Apache, MySQL, and PHP to bring form to the function of Asterisk. Before we dive into the heart of administering a FreePBX system, we have a few steps to complete in order to install and configure these frameworks. Though going from a fresh Linux install to a working Asterisk and FreePBX phone server is a relatively straightforward process, it is advisable to be careful. The steps in this chapter form the foundation of your server and their successful completion is critical to the stability of your Asterisk and FreePBX installations.

While every deployment is going to be different and have different requirements, the steps in this chapter will provide installation instructions for CentOS 5.2 and Ubuntu Server 8.10.

Installing FreePBX on CentOS 5.2

The **Community ENTerprise Operating System (CentOS)** is a secure, stable OS based on Red Hat Enterprise Linux. CentOS is a popular choice for Asterisk/FreePBX systems. CentOS 5.2 should be installed with the following packages selected:

- Applications
  - Editors
  - Text-based Internet
- Development
  - Development Libraries
  - Development Tools

- Servers
    - ○ DNS
    - ○ Mail Server
    - ○ MySQL Database Server
    - ○ Server Configuration Tools
    - ○ Web Server
- Base System
    - ○ Administration Tools
    - ○ Base

All of the other groups and packages should be unchecked during installation, as they are not required and may have an impact on the performance. SELinux should also be disabled during CentOS installation.

Once you have a clean CentOS 5.2 install to work from, the prerequisite packages can be installed.

Prerequisite packages

FreePBX requires several prerequisite packages for being installed and functioning properly. Most prerequisite packages are not included in standard Linux distribution installations, but all of them should be available in your distribution's package management system.

The first important step is to update your system, ensuring that all security updates are installed and that all the installed packages are at their latest version. To update all the installed packages on CentOS 5.2, log in as root and type the following command into the system console:

```
yum update -y
```

The system will proceed to download and install any packages that have been updated since the release of your operating system. Depending on how many updates are required and the speed of your Internet connection, this process can take anywhere from a few minutes to several hours.

Once the system is fully up to date, it is a good idea to reboot so that the updated services can restart, and newer kernels can be booted. In order to reboot, type the following into the console:

```
shutdown -r now
```

Now that the system is up to date, the required prerequisite libraries and packages can be installed. As long as the correct base packages were selected during the installation of CentOS, FreePBX will only require the following additional packages:

Package	Purpose
LibTIFF development headers	Used for dynamic generation of images (such as call usage graphs)
PHP GD library	As with LibTIFF, the GD libraries are used by PHP to dynamically generate images
PHP MySQL library	Allows FreePBX to read and write to its MySQL database backend
Kernel or SMP kernel development headers	Used to allow DAHDI to build its modules against the running kernel
Audio file development headers	Allows FreePBX to transcode recordings and music-on-hold files when they are uploaded
MySQL development headers	These headers are required when building applications that use MySQL databases (FreePBX is based on a MySQL database backend)

To install the required prerequisite packages for CentOS 5.2, log in as root and type the following:

```
yum install libtiff-devel php-gd php-mysql php-pear kernel-devel kernel-
smp-devel audiofile-devel mysql-devel -y
```

 Note that all of the above is a single yum command, and should be typed as if it was written on a single line.

Now that all of the prerequisite packages are installed, we can install Asterisk. First, switch to the /usr/src directory by typing the following into the console:

```
cd /usr/src
```

Install Asterisk from source

Many Linux distributions provide Asterisk and its dependent libraries in their package management systems. It is recommended that Asterisk, Asterisk-Addons, LibPRI, and Zaptel should always be compiled and installed from source. This avoids improperly built or outdated installations.

A core Asterisk installation consists of four components—Asterisk, Asterisk-Addons, DAHDI, and LibPRI:

- "Asterisk" is the main Asterisk routing engine
- Asterisk-Addons component contains commonly used Asterisk applications (such as the application that writes CDR records to a MySQL database, which FreePBX uses)
- **DAHDI** is the **Digium Asterisk Hardware Device Interface** package, which allows Asterisk to communicate with additional telephony hardware devices (such as analog trunk cards)
- The LibPRI package enables Asterisk to interface with PRI, BRI, and QSIG trunks

Type the following into the console to download the source code for Asterisk, Asterisk-Addons, DAHDI, and LibPRI:

```
wget http://downloads.digium.com/pub/asterisk/asterisk-1.4-current.tar.gz
```

```
wget http://downloads.digium.com/pub/asterisk/asterisk-addons-1.4-
current.tar.gz
```

```
wget http://downloads.digium.com/pub/telephony/dahdi-linux-complete/
dahdi-linux-complete-current.tar.gz
```

```
wget http://downloads.digium.com/pub/libpri/libpri-1.4-current.tar.gz
```

Extract the source code:

```
tar zxf asterisk-1.4-current.tar.gz
```

```
tar zxf asterisk-addons-1.4-current.tar.gz
```

```
tar zxf dahdi-linux-complete-current.tar.gz
```

```
tar zxf libpri-1.4-current.tar.gz
```

Compile and install the DAHDI telephony hardware interface modules:

```
cd dahdi-linux-complete-2.*
make all
make install
make config
```

Compile and install Asterisk with the following commands:

```
cd ../asterisk-1.4.*
./configure
make install
make samples
```

Compile and install the Asterisk-Addons modules (contains the application that FreePBX uses to write call detail records to the MySQL database):

```
cd ../asterisk-addons-1.4.*
./configure
make install
```

Compile and install the LibPRI modules for PRI, BRI, and QSIG interface support:

```
cd ../libpri-1.4.*
make
make install
```

PHP Extension and Application Repository (PEAR) is a repository and distribution system for various reusable PHP libraries. PEAR contains a module called "DB", which abstracts calls away from a particular database engine (allowing the same database code to be used against different database backends). FreePBX uses the PEAR DB module to allow its code to be used with both MySQL and PostgreSQL currently (with the possibility of additional database engines in the future). The module is installed through PEAR by typing the following into the console:

```
pear install db
```

The final prerequisite is the LAME MP3 encoder. LAME is left out of the CentOS package management system. So, like Asterisk, it should be compiled from source. The latest version of LAME can be found by visiting the site http://lame. sourceforge.net/. If the latest version is newer than 3.98.2, then the newer version should be used instead. Type the following into the console to switch to the /usr/src directory and download LAME:

```
cd /usr/src
```

```
wget http://superb-east.dl.sourceforge.net/sourceforge/lame/lame-398-2.tar.gz
```

Extract LAME using the following command:

```
tar zxf lame-398-2.tar.gz
```

Compile and install LAME:

```
cd lame-398-2
./configure
make
make install
```

Finally, we start Asterisk as a background process by typing the following into the console:

```
asterisk &
```

Note that this method of starting Asterisk is only temporary. Once installed, the FreePBX startup script will be configured to start at boot.

Setting up the database

FreePBX utilizes a MySQL database to store all the configurations shown in the web interface it provides.

Under CentOS 5.2, the MySQL engine is neither started nor set up to start at boot. We must first start the MySQL database engine and then set it to start at boot time. If this is not done, not only will MySQL have to be manually started each time the system needs to be administered, but also the system will not log any calls (all CDRs are written to a MySQL database):

```
/etc/init.d/mysqld start
chkconfig mysqld on
```

A root password must be set for MySQL. The root MySQL user has full administrative access to all of the databases on the system. Therefore, leaving the root password blank leaves a very large security hole:

```
mysqladmin -u root password newpassword
```

Replace newpassword with the password you would like to set for the MySQL root user.

A separate user account under which Asterisk can run should also be created. It is common for Asterisk to run as the root user on a system (and that is usually an easier way to make things work), but this is a security risk. Should Asterisk or Apache be compromised by a remote exploit, the flaw cannot be used to take over the entire server when Asterisk runs as its own user. Create a user account called asterisk that Asterisk will run as, using the following command:

```
useradd -c "Asterisk PBX" -d /var/lib/asterisk asterisk
```

Use the mysqladmin command to create a database to store Asterisk configuration and another to store call detail records:

```
mysqladmin -u root -p create asterisk
mysqladmin -u root -p create asteriskcdrdb
```

Enter your MySQL root password when prompted.

FreePBX has created "prepared SQL statements" to set up the structure of each database it uses. Type the following to switch to the /usr/src directory and download the FreePBX installer archive:

```
cd /usr/src
wget http://internap.dl.sourceforge.net/sourceforge/amportal/freepbx-
2.5.1.tar.gz
```

The above command will download FreePBX version 2.5.1. To check for the current version of FreePBX, visit http://freepbx.org/download-freepbx. The current version will be listed next to the **Download FreePBX** button. If the listed version is newer than 2.5.1, it should be used instead.

Extract FreePBX:

```
tar zxf freepbx-2.5.1.tar.gz
```

Switch to the FreePBX SQL directory:

```
cd freepbx-2.5.1/SQL
```

The two prepared statements provided by FreePBX are newinstall.sql and cdr_mysql_table.sql. The newinstall.sql file contains the necessary SQL statements to create the tables that store all of the FreePBX configuration data (extensions, call targets, call routing information, and so on). The cd_mysql_table.sql file contains one single statement that creates a CDR table for storing all call detail records. To run the SQL statements contained in these files, type the following commands into the console:

```
mysql -u root -p asterisk < newinstall.sql
mysql -u root -p asteriskcdrdb < cdr_mysql_table.sql
```

Enter your MySQL root password when prompted.

Now we must grant the Asterisk user permissions on the Asterisk and Asterisk CDR databases. FreePBX will not function without this access. To grant permissions, we must first drop to a MySQL shell as follows:

```
mysql -u root -p
```

Enter your MySQL root password when prompted.

Once at the MySQL shell, type the following commands to grant the appropriate privileges to the Asterisk user. Remember to replace `freepbxdbpassword` with a password of your choice, and note that the password should be *enclosed in single quotes*.

```
mysql> GRANT ALL PRIVILEGES ON asterisk.* TO asterisk@localhost
IDENTIFIED BY 'freepbxdbpassword';

mysql> GRANT ALL PRIVILEGES ON asteriskcdrdb.* TO asterisk@localhost
IDENTIFIED BY 'freepbxdbpassword';

mysql> flush privileges;

mysql> \q
```

Setting up file permissions

The final installation step is to set up appropriate permissions and general configurations. To make the required configuration changes, the following examples make use of the `sed` command. The `sed` command can take a stream of input and rewrite it on the fly based on patterns listed in the command. The syntax for the following `sed` commands used works as follows:

```
sed -i "s/pattern_to_find/replacement_pattern/" /path/to/file
```

The `-i` option tells `sed` to edit the input file in place, such that the listed file is changed and a new file with the requested changes is not created in its place.

The `s/` tells `sed` that we are looking to replace a specific pattern with text of our own.

The `pattern_to_find` token should be replaced by the text that we are searching for. This can be a normal alphanumeric pattern, or a regular expression.

The `replacement_pattern` token should be replaced with the value that we want to replace the `pattern_to_find` token with.

As FreePBX will need to interact with Asterisk, the Apache web server must be set up to run as the `asterisk` user. To change the user and the group that Apache runs as, enter the following commands as the root user:

```
sed -i "s/User apache/User asterisk/" /etc/httpd/conf/httpd.conf
sed -i "s/Group apache/Group asterisk/" /etc/httpd/conf/httpd.conf
```

We must also allow FreePBX to override various default Apache directives. To allow the directive overrides, type the following into the console:

```
sed -i "s/AllowOverride None/AllowOverride All/"
/etc/httpd/conf/httpd.conf
```

The Asterisk run directory (where the Asterisk PID file will be stored) should be changed to /var/run/asterisk:

```
sed -i "s/astrundir => \/var\/run/astrundir => \/var\/run\/asterisk/" /
etc/asterisk/asterisk.conf
```

We must also create the /var/run/asterisk directory so that Asterisk can write its PID file there (as we have just configured it to):

```
mkdir /var/run/asterisk
```

PHP will need to be configured to allow for large file uploads up to 20 MB, as FreePBX modules can reach above the default 8 MB limit. To change the PHP limits, type the following into the console:

```
sed -i "s/post_max_size = 8M/post_max_size = 20M/" /etc/php.ini
sed -i "s/upload_max_filesize = 2M/upload_max_filesize = 20M/" /etc/php.
ini
```

Finally, the asterisk user should be set up as the owner of several directories that Asterisk will use during the normal operation:

```
chown -R asterisk:asterisk /var/spool/asterisk/
chown -R asterisk:asterisk /var/log/asterisk/
chown -R asterisk:asterisk /var/run/asterisk/
```

At this point, all packages should be installed and configured correctly. It is recommended that your server be rebooted now, to allow all the changes to take effect.

FreePBX base installation

Now that we have a working Linux install, all the prerequisite packages, and a functioning MySQL database, we can finally install FreePBX. As FreePBX has already been downloaded, the process is simply to switch to the FreePBX directory and run the installer:

```
cd /usr/src/freepbx-2.5.1
./install_amp install
```

You will be asked a series of configuration questions that the installer uses to generate a configuration file located at /etc/amportal.conf. If a mistake is made during the question and answer part of the installation, simply remove this file using the following command, and run the install_amp install command once again:

```
rm -f /etc/amportal.conf
```

Question	Suggested answer
Enter your USERNAME to connect to the 'asterisk' database	This is the username you set up with permissions on the Asterisk database and is simply called asterisk. Type "asterisk" and hit the *Enter* key.
Enter your PASSWORD to connect to the 'asterisk' database	This is the password you set up during the grant all privileges step for the Asterisk database. Type your password and hit the *Enter* key.
Enter the hostname of 'asterisk' database	This is the location of your MySQL server. Using the setup listed in this book, this will be localhost (as the MySQL server resides on the same server as the Apache server). If the MySQL server resides on a different server than Apache, the answer to this question should be the hostname or IP address of the server where MySQL resides. Type the hostname or IP address of the server running MySQL and hit the *Enter* key.
Enter a USERNAME to connect to the Asterisk Manager Interface	Pick a username that FreePBX can use to communicate with the Asterisk Manager Interface. Leaving this as "admin" is fine. Type the desired username and press the *Enter* key.
Enter a PASSWORD to connect to the Asterisk Manager Interface	Pick a password that FreePBX will use when communicating with the Asterisk Manager Interface. It is strongly recommended that the password be changed from the default of amp111. Type your desired password and press the *Enter* key.
Enter the path to use for your AMP web root	This is the location of your Apache root folder. By default, CentOS 5.2 will place this in /var/www/html. Type your web root and press the *Enter* key.
Enter the IP ADDRESS or hostname used to access the AMP web-admin	It is the IP address or hostname that you have assigned to your Asterisk server. It is usually the IP address that you will type into your browser to view the FreePBX web interface, when you are ready to configure your Asterisk PBX. Type your IP address or hostname and press the *Enter* key.

Question	Suggested answer
Enter a PASSWORD to perform call transfers with the Flash Operator Panel	The **Flash Operator Panel** is a visual switchboard that allows you to view activity on your PBX, as well as bridge, transfer, or disconnect calls. It is strongly recommended that you change this default password value. Type your desired password and press the *Enter* key.
Use simple Extensions [extensions] admin or separate Devices and Users [deviceanduser]	FreePBX can associate one user to one device (extensions mode) or one user to many devices (deviceanduser mode). This value can always be changed at any time, and the differences will be discussed later in this book. For now, it is recommended to leave the default value of extensions and hit the *Enter* key.
Enter directory in which to store AMP executable scripts	This is the directory in which FreePBX will store any script that executes against the system. Unless your system calls for a specific change to this location, it is recommended to leave this at the default value of /var/lib/asterisk/bin and press the *Enter* key.
Enter directory in which to store super-user scripts	This is the directory in which FreePBX will store any scripts that execute against the system with root privileges. As with the previous configuration question, unless your setup calls for a specific change to this value, leave it at the default of /usr/local/sbin and press the *Enter* key.

At this point, the FreePBX installer will run through the rest of the installation process automatically. As the final step, we need to configure FreePBX to start automatically when the system boots:

```
echo "/usr/local/sbin/amportal start" >> /etc/rc.local
```

Installing FreePBX on Ubuntu Server 8.10

Ubuntu Server is a popular and stable operating system based on Debian GNU/Linux. It is becoming increasingly popular for general-purpose server deployments, and is a good choice for an Asterisk/FreePBX server.

Ubuntu Server 8.10 should be installed with the following options:

- DNS server
- LAMP server
- Mail server
- OpenSSH server

Once you have a clean Ubuntu Server 8.10 install to work from, the prerequisite packages can be installed.

Prerequisite packages

FreePBX requires several prerequisite packages to install and function properly. Most prerequisite packages are not included in standard Linux distribution installations, but all should be available in your distributions package management system.

The first important step is to update your system, ensuring that all security updates are installed and all installed packages are at the latest version. To update all of the installed packages on Ubuntu Server 8.10, log in as the standard user that you created during the setup, and type the following into the system console:

```
sudo aptitude update
```
```
sudo aptitude upgrade -y
```

Enter your user account password when prompted.

The system will proceed to download and install any of the packages that have been updated since the release of your operating system. Depending on how many updates are required and the speed of your Internet connection, this process can take anything from a few minutes to several hours.

Once the system is fully up to date, it is a good idea to reboot so that the updated services can restart and newer kernels can be booted. To reboot, type the following into the console:

```
sudo reboot
```

Now that the system is up to date, the required prerequisite libraries and packages can be installed. To install the required prerequisite packages on Ubuntu Server 8.10, log in as a standard user and type the following:

```
sudo aptitude install build-essential autoconf automake libtool flex
bison libssl-dev libnewt-dev libncurses5-dev linux-headers-$(uname -r)
sox curl mysql-client libmysqlclient-dev php5 php5-cli php5-gd php5-curl
php5-mcrypt php5-xmlrpc php5-mhash php5-suhosin php5-common php5-xsl
libapache2-mod-php5 php-pear lame subversion -y
```

Note that all of the above is a single `aptitude` command, and should be typed as if it was written on a single line.

Now that all prerequisite packages are installed, we can install Asterisk.

First, switch to the `/usr/src` directory by typing the following into the console:

```
cd /usr/src
```

Install Asterisk from source

Many Linux distributions provide Asterisk and its dependent libraries in their package management systems. It is recommended that Asterisk, Asterisk-Addons, LibPRI, and Zaptel always be compiled and installed from source. This avoids improperly built or outdated installations.

A core Asterisk installation consists of four components—Asterisk, Asterisk-Addons, DAHDI, and LibPRI:

- "Asterisk" is the main Asterisk routing engine
- Asterisk-Addons component contains commonly used Asterisk applications (such as the application that writes CDR records to a MySQL database, which FreePBX uses)
- **DAHDI** is the **Digium Asterisk Hardware Device Interface** package, which allows Asterisk to communicate with additional telephony hardware devices (such as analog trunk cards)
- The LibPRI package enables Asterisk to interface with PRI, BRI, and QSIG trunks

Type the following into the console to download the source code for Asterisk, Asterisk-Addons, DAHDI, and LibPRI:

```
sudo wget http://downloads.digium.com/pub/asterisk/asterisk-1.4-current.
tar.gz
```

```
sudo wget http://downloads.digium.com/pub/asterisk/asterisk-addons-1.4-
current.tar.gz
```

```
sudo wget http://downloads.digium.com/pub/telephony/dahdi-linux-complete/
dahdi-linux-complete-current.tar.gz
```

```
sudo wget http://downloads.digium.com/pub/libpri/libpri-1.4-current.
tar.gz
```

Extract the source code:

```
sudo tar zxf asterisk-1.4-current.tar.gz

sudo tar zxf asterisk-addons-1.4-current.tar.gz

sudo tar zxf zaptel-1.4-current.tar.gz

sudo tar zxf libpri-1.4-current.tar.gz
```

Compile and install the DAHDI telephony hardware interface modules:

```
cd dahdi-linux-complete-2.*
sudo make all
sudo make install
make config
```

Compile and install Asterisk:

```
cd ../asterisk-1.4.*
./configure
sudo make install
make samples
```

Compile and install the Asterisk-Addons modules:

```
cd ../asterisk-addons-1.4.*
./configure
sudo make install
```

Compile and install the LibPRI modules:

```
cd ../libpri-1.4.*
make
sudo make install
```

The PEAR DB module is installed through PEAR software by typing the following into the console:

```
pear install db
```

Finally, we start Asterisk as a background process by typing:

```
asterisk &
```

Note that this method of starting Asterisk is only temporary. Once installed, the FreePBX startup script will be configured to run at boot.

Setting up the database

FreePBX utilizes a MySQL database to store all of the configurations shown in the web interface it provides.

Under Ubuntu Server 8.10, MySQL must simply be started. A MySQL root password is entered during the Ubuntu install process, and Ubuntu automatically sets up the MySQL service to start at boot time. To start MySQL, type the following command:

```
/etc/init.d/invoke-rc.d mysql start
```

A separate user account under which Asterisk can run should also be created. It is common for Asterisk to run as the root user on a system (and almost always an easier way to make things work), but it is a security risk. Should Asterisk or Apache be compromised by a remote exploit, the flaw cannot be used to take over the entire server when Asterisk runs as its own user. Create a user account called asterisk that Asterisk will run as, using the following command:

```
adduser -gecos "Asterisk PBX" --home /var/lib/asterisk --system --group
asterisk
```

 Note that all of the above is a single adduser command, and should be typed as if it was written on a single line.

Create a database to store Asterisk configuration and another to store call detail records:

```
mysqladmin -u root -p create asterisk
```

```
mysqladmin -u root -p create asteriskcdrdb
```

Enter your MySQL root password when prompted.

FreePBX has created prepared SQL statements to set up the structure of each database it uses. Type the following to switch to the /usr/src directory and download the FreePBX installer archive:

```
cd /usr/src
```

```
sudo wget http://internap.dl.sourceforge.net/sourceforge/amportal/
freepbx-2.5.1.tar.gz
```

The above command will download FreePBX version 2.5.1. To check for the current version of FreePBX, visit the site http://freepbx.org/download-freepbx. The current version will be listed next to the **Download FreePBX** button. If the listed version is newer than 2.5.1, it should be used instead.

Extract FreePBX using the following command:

```
tar zxf freepbx-2.5.1.tar.gz
```

Switch to the FreePBX SQL directory:

```
cd freepbx-2.5.1/SQL
```

The two prepared statements provided by FreePBX are `newinstall.sql` and `cdr_mysql_table.sql`. The `newinstall.sql` file contains the necessary SQL statements to create the tables that store all FreePBX configuration data (extensions, call targets, call routing information, etc.). The cd_mysql_table.sql file contains one single statement that creates a CDR table for storing all call details records. To run the SQL statements contained in these files, run the following commands:

```
mysql -u root -p asterisk < newinstall.sql
```

```
mysql -u root -p asteriskcdrdb < cdr_mysql_table.sql
```

Enter your MySQL root password when prompted.

Now we must grant the Asterisk user permissions on the Asterisk and Asterisk CDR databases. FreePBX will not function without this access. To grant permissions, we must first drop to a MySQL shell:

```
mysql -u root -p
```

Enter your MySQL root password when prompted.

Once at the MySQL shell, type the following commands to grant the appropriate privileges to the Asterisk user. Remember to replace `freepbxdbpassword` with a password of your choice and note that the password should be *enclosed in single quotes*.

```
mysql> GRANT ALL PRIVILEGES ON asterisk.* TO asterisk@localhost
IDENTIFIED BY 'freepbxdbpassword';
```

```
mysql> GRANT ALL PRIVILEGES ON asteriskcdrdb.* TO asterisk@localhost
IDENTIFIED BY 'freepbxdbpassword';
```

```
mysql> flush privileges;
```

```
mysql> \q
```

Setting up file permissions

The final installation step is to set up appropriate permissions and general configurations. To make the required configuration changes, the examples shown as follows make use of the `sed` command. The `sed` command can take a stream of input and rewrite it on the fly based on patterns listed in the command. The syntax for the following `sed` commands used works as follows:

```
sed -i "s/pattern_to_find/replacement_pattern/" /path/to/file
```

The `-i` option tells `sed` to edit the input file in place, such that the listed file is changed and a new file with the requested changes is not created in its place.

The `s/` tells `sed` that we are looking to replace a specific pattern with text of our own.

The `pattern_to_find` token should be replaced by the text that we are searching for. This can be a normal alphanumeric pattern, or a regular expression.

The `replacement_pattern` token should be replaced with the value that we want to replace the `pattern_to_find` token with.

As FreePBX will need to interact with Asterisk, the Apache web server must be set up to run as the `asterisk` user. To change the user and the group that Apache runs as, enter the following commands as the root user:

```
sed -i "s/www-data/asterisk/" /etc/apache2/envvars
```

We must also allow FreePBX to override various default Apache directives. To allow the directive overrides, type the following into the console:

```
sed -i "s/AllowOverride None/AllowOverride All/" /etc/apache2/apache2.conf
```

The Asterisk run directory (where the Asterisk PID file will be stored) should be changed to /var/run/asterisk:

```
sed -i "s/astrundir => \/var\/run/astrundir => \/var\/run\/asterisk/" /etc/asterisk/asterisk.conf
```

PHP will need to be configured to allow for large file uploads up to 20 MB, as FreePBX modules can reach above the default 8 MB limit. To change the PHP limits type the following:

```
sed -i "s/post_max_size = 8M/post_max_size = 20M/" /etc/php5/apache2/php.ini
```

```
sed -i "s/upload_max_filesize = 2M/upload_max_filesize = 20M/" /etc/php5/apache2/php.ini
```

The Asterisk run directory (where the process ID file is stored) is located on a temporary file system under Ubuntu. Each time the server reboots, the directory will disappear along with its associated permissions. To correct this, the directory must be created and permissions set at boot time:

```
echo "mkdir /var/run/asterisk" >> /etc/rc.local
```

```
echo "chown -R asterisk:asterisk /var/run/asterisk" >> /etc/rc.local
```

Note that the chown statement as above is one command and should be typed on a single line.

Finally, the asterisk user should be set up as the owner of several directories that Asterisk will use during normal operation:

```
chown -R asterisk:asterisk /var/spool/asterisk/
chown -R asterisk:asterisk /var/log/asterisk/
```

At this point, all packages should be installed and configured correctly. It is recommended that your server be rebooted now to allow all changes to take effect.

FreePBX base installation

Now that we have a working Linux install, all prerequisite packages, and a functioning MySQL database, we can finally install FreePBX. As FreePBX has already been downloaded, the process is simply to switch to the FreePBX directory and run the installer:

```
cd /usr/src/freepbx-2.5.1
./install_amp install
```

You will be asked a series of configuration questions that the installer uses to generate a configuration file located at /etc/amportal.conf. If a mistake is made during the question and answer part of the installation, simply remove this file using the following command, and run the install_amp install command:

```
rm -f /etc/amportal.conf
```

Question	Suggested answer
Enter your USERNAME to connect to the 'asterisk' database	The username we set up with permissions on the asterisk database is simply called asterisk. Type "asterisk" and hit the *Enter* key.
Enter your PASSWORD to connect to the 'asterisk' database	This is the password that you setup during the grant all privileges step for the Asterisk database. Type your password and hit the *Enter* key.

Question	Suggested answer
`Enter the hostname of 'asterisk' database`	This is the location of your MySQL server. Using the setup listed in this book, this will be `localhost` (as the MySQL server resides on the same server as the Apache server does). If the MySQL server resides on a different server than Apache, the answer to this question should be the hostname or IP address of the server where MySQL resides. Type the hostname or IP address of the server running MySQL and hit the *Enter* key.
`Enter a USERNAME to connect to the Asterisk Manager Interface`	Pick a username that FreePBX can use to communicate with the Asterisk Manager Interface. Leaving this as "admin" is fine. Type the desired username and press the *Enter* key.
`Enter a PASSWORD to connect to the Asterisk Manager Interface`	Pick a password that FreePBX will use when communicating with the Asterisk Manager Interface. It is strongly recommended that the password be changed from the default of "amp111". Type your desired password and press the *Enter* key.
`Enter the path to use for your AMP web root`	This is the location of your Apache root folder. By default, Ubuntu Server 8.10 will place this in `/var/www`. Type your web root and press the Enter key.
`Enter the IP ADDRESS or hostname used to access the AMP web-admin`	This is the IP address or hostname that you have assigned to your Asterisk server. This is usually the IP address that you will type into your browser to view the FreePBX web interface when you are ready to configure your Asterisk PBX. Type your IP address or hostname and press the *Enter* key.
`Enter a PASSWORD to perform call transfers with the Flash Operator Panel`	The **Flash Operator Panel** is a visual switchboard that allows you to view activity on your PBX, as well as bridge, transfer, or disconnect calls. It is strongly recommended that you change this default password value. Type your desired password and press the *Enter* key.

Question	Suggested answer
Use simple Extensions [extensions] admin or separate Devices and Users [deviceanduser]	FreePBX can associate one user to one device (extensions mode) or one user to many devices (deviceanduser mode). This value can always be changed at any time, and the differences will be discussed later in this book. For now, it is recommended to leave the default value of "extensions" and push the *Enter* key.
Enter directory in which to store AMP executable scripts	This is the directory in which FreePBX will store any scripts that execute against the system. Unless your system calls for a specific change to this location, it is recommended to leave this at the default value of /var/lib/ asterisk/bin and press the *Enter* key.

At this point, the FreePBX installer will run through the rest of the install process automatically. As the final step, we need to configure FreePBX to start automatically when the system boots:

```
echo "/usr/sbin/amportal start &" > /etc/rc.local
```

Summary

By now, we should have a fully functional Linux server running Apache, MySQL, Asterisk, and FreePBX. Asterisk should be running under a dedicated user account for additional security. Congratulations! Installation is often the most difficult part of configuring a FreePBX system.

In the next chapter, we delve into the ins and outs of maintaining a FreePBX system by learning about installing, removing, and updating modules.

2
Module Maintenance

On its own, the core FreePBX installation is just a framework. Every function performed by FreePBX, from inbound routing to voicemail, is provided by a module that plugs into this framework. FreePBX provides more than fifty modules, each providing a specific set of functions. When administering a FreePBX system, Apache serves as a web interface for each module. The modules store their configuration in a database, which the FreePBX framework processes and then writes out to the Asterisk configuration files. The configuration files are read by Asterisk, making the configuration from the FreePBX modules live. This process is shown in the following figure:

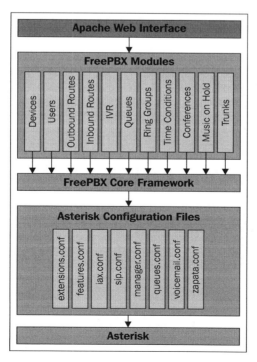

Everything in FreePBX is a module, including the base components—Core Framework, Localizations, Asterisk Recording Interface, and Flash Operator Panel. This modularized structure is how new features are added to the system, as well as how updates are installed.

Splitting of functionality into modules also allows each installation of FreePBX to be built specifically for its deployment requirements. If a PBX simply needs to store voicemail for users, all it will require is the inbound routing and voicemail modules. A PBX that answers calls and then routes them to another PBX may just require the inbound routing and outbound routing modules. Installing just the required modules simplifies administration and improves startup and reload times.

Modules can specify dependencies, allowing each module to be as small and efficient as possible, by building on the shoulders of previously created modules. All of the modules will generally have at least one dependency.

To get us started with module management, this chapter will discuss the following:

- Updating existing modules from the online repository
- Installing new modules from the online repository
- Installing and updating modules from a file

Updating modules from the online repository

The usual installation method for new modules or system updates for FreePBX comes from the FreePBX module repository. The module repository is hosted by FreePBX's partners and sponsors. Access to the repository is free.

The following instructions walk through the process of updating modules. As with any system update, there is always the possibility of negative consequences when an update is applied. It is a good idea to back up the system prior to installing updates (please see Chapter 10, *System Protection, Backup and Restoration* for information on backup). Note that the built-in FreePBX backup software will not be available after a fresh installation. However, it is not required as there is no configuration that needs to be backed up yet.

From a fresh installation of FreePBX, only the core set of modules will be installed, but they may require updates prior to proceeding with any further configuration. To go from a fresh installation to a fully-functional PBX, we must first update any core modules that are out of date and then proceed with the installation of additional, optional modules.

1. First, we log in to our FreePBX installation by entering the IP address of our Asterisk server into the address bar of our web browser. We should see the FreePBX welcome screen as follows:

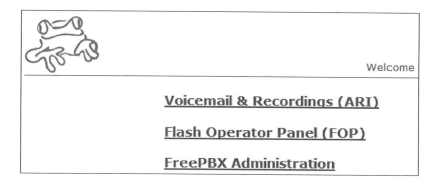

2. Click on the **FreePBX Administration** link, as shown in the previous screenshot, in order to begin administering FreePBX. The main FreePBX screen will prompt for configuration changes to be applied using an orange-colored button at the top of the screen. Do not apply these settings until the core modules have been installed and updated.

Important: Do not apply configuration changes before module installation

A fresh installation of FreePBX will prompt for configuration settings to be applied as soon as anyone logs into the system. It is important not to click on the orange-colored **Apply Configuration Changes** bar before properly installing modules in the required order. Applying configuration settings before core modules are installed and updated could result in a broken, unusable system.

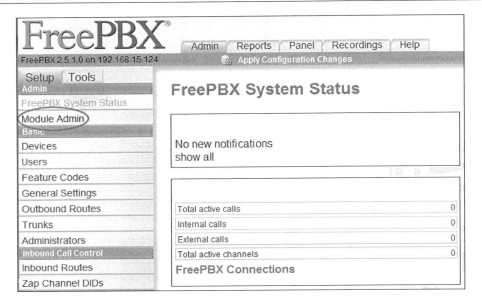

3. Click on the **Module Admin** link in the navigation menu on the left, as shown in the previous screenshot, in order to enter the module management screen:

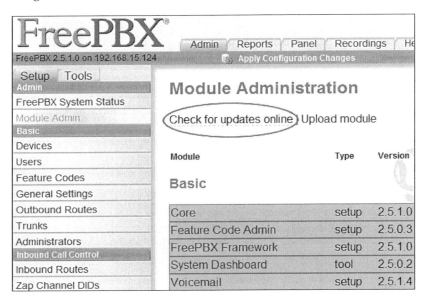

4. Click on the **Check for updates online** link, as shown in the previous screenshot, in order to have FreePBX check the online module repository for new and updated modules. A list of all of the available modules, their versions, and installation status will be displayed as follows:

Basic			
Core	setup	2.5.1.0	Online upgrade available (2.5.1.5)
Feature Code Admin	setup	2.5.0.3	Online upgrade available (2.5.0.4)
FreePBX ARI Framework	setup		Not Installed (Available online: 2.5.2.1)
FreePBX FOP Framework	setup		Not Installed (Available online: 2.5.0.1)
FreePBX Framework	setup	2.5.1.0	Online upgrade available (2.5.1.1)
FreePBX Localization Updates	setup		Not Installed (Available online: 2.5.1.2)
System Dashboard	tool	2.5.0.2	Online upgrade available (2.5.0.6)
Voicemail	setup	2.5.1.4	Online upgrade available (2.5.1.6)
CID & Number Management			
Phonebook Directory	tool		Not Installed (Available online: 2.5.0.1)
Speed Dial Functions	module		Not Installed (Available online: 2.5.0.1)

5. Clicking on the name of a module will provide upgrade or installation actions for the module, a description of the functions that the module provides, and a changelog that lists the development updates that were applied to each of the previous versions of the module as shown in the following screenshot. Keep in mind that a module update may fix a bug that has been worked around, or may alter the way a module works. When updating a module, it is important to examine the changelog in order to understand what impact the update will have on the running system.

Feature Code Admin	setup	2.5.0.3	Online upgrade available (2.5.0.4)
FreePBX ARI Framework	setup		Not Installed (Available online: 2.5.2.1)
Action	Description for version 2.5.2.1		
Description			
Changelog	This module provides a facility to install bug fixes to the ARI code that is not otherwise housed in a module, it used to be part of framework but has been removed to isolate ARI from Framework updates.		
FreePBX FOP Framework	setup		Not Installed (Available online: 2.5.0.1)
FreePBX Framework	setup	2.5.1.0	Online upgrade available (2.5.1.1)
FreePBX Localization Updates	setup		Not Installed (Available online: 2.5.1.2)

The **Action** tab shows radio buttons to change what will happen with that particular module when the **Process** button is clicked on, as shown in the next screenshot. The Process button is located both above and below the list of modules on the righthand side of the screen. The **No Action** option will leave that module intact; no changes will occur. If the module is not already installed, **Download and Install** will perform the necessary steps to obtain and install the module. If a module is already installed and an upgrade is available, **Download and Upgrade** will perform the necessary steps to preserve old configurations, update the module to the latest available version, and update old configuration schemas if necessary.

 The module upgrade page contains an **Upgrade All** link that selects all of the modules with available upgrades. This link should not be used until the **Core** and **FreePBX Framework** modules have first been updated.

6. After a fresh install of FreePBX, check the status of the **Core** module. If the module status is showing **Online upgrade available** in red text as shown in the following screenshot, then this module should be updated first. Click on the module name, click on the **Action** tab, and click on the **Download and Upgrade** radio button:

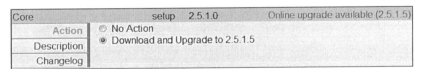

7. Click on the **Process** button on the right side of the screen to begin the upgrade process. FreePBX will prompt for confirmation. In order to continue click on the **Confirm** button as shown in the following screenshot:

8. Once the **Confirm** button has been clicked on, FreePBX will begin to update the requested module as shown in the following screenshot. Update status will be shown in a small overlay window. Any noteworthy status messages or errors will be displayed here. An error during module operations could cause certain features of your PBX to stop functioning correctly. Therefore, be sure you examine the contents of this window carefully, and resolve any errors that are listed.

> Receiving errors when updating or installing modules is rare. An error during module processing is almost always the result of a manual change that has been made to the FreePBX configuration file, or to the FreePBX database. If an error is received at this stage, verify that any manual changes to /etc/amportal. conf since installation have been reversed. The original database schema can be restored by re-running the database setup portion of the FreePBX installation, if necessary.

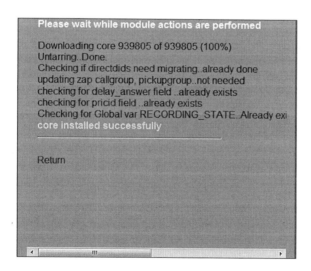

9. When updates are complete, click on the **Return** link in the overlay window, as shown in the previous screenshot, in order to return to the module administration page. Once the **Core** module is updated, it is a good idea to update the FreePBX Framework module in the same manner as the **Core** module. Click on **Check for updates online**, click on the **FreePBX Framework** header, select the **Download and Upgrade** option, and click on the **Process** button.

10. Click on the **Confirm** button to upgrade the framework module.

11. Once the **Core** and **FreePBX Framework** modules have been updated, any other installed modules can be upgraded. All of the outdated modules can be updated in a single step by clicking on the **Upgrade All** link in the top right corner of the online module repository page, and then clicking on the **Process** button.

12. Once all of the modules are up to date, we can finally proceed with applying configuration changes. Clicking on the orange-colored **Apply Configuration Changes** bar at the top of the screen as shown in the following screenshot, will take all of the configuration data stored in the FreePBX MySQL database, write it out to the appropriate Asterisk configuration files, and then force Asterisk to load the new configuration into memory. To start this process, click on the orange-colored bar. A confirmation overlay window will appear:

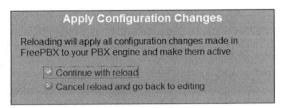

13. Click on the **Continue with reload** link, as shown in the previous screenshot, in order to proceed. The overlay will disappear once the reload process is complete.

All of the module updates follow the same process of selecting the module, selecting the **Download and Upgrade** option, and clicking on the **Process** button. The FreePBX developers publish updates frequently. It is recommended that you check for updates once a month to ensure that your PBX is always running the latest version of any installed module.

Installing new modules from the online repository

FreePBX provides more than fifty installable modules that can add new features or functionality to our PBX. Installing modules from the online repository follows a very similar process to updating modules from the online repository.

1. From any page within the FreePBX interface, click on the **Module Admin** link in the menu on the left. The **Module Admin** link is present on both the **Setup** and **Tools** tabs.

2. From the module administration page, click on the **Check for updates online** link. FreePBX will compare the list of currently installed modules (and their versions) against the latest list of available modules in the online repository. We should be presented with a list of all available modules as follows:

Basic			
Core	setup	2.5.1.5	Enabled and up to date
Feature Code Admin	setup	2.5.0.4	Enabled and up to date
FreePBX ARI Framework	setup		Not Installed (Available online: 2.5.2.1)
FreePBX FOP Framework	setup		Not Installed (Available online: 2.5.0.1)
FreePBX Framework	setup	2.5.1.1	Enabled and up to date
FreePBX Localization Updates	setup		Not Installed (Available online: 2.5.1.2)
System Dashboard	tool	2.5.0.6	Enabled and up to date
Voicemail	setup	2.5.1.6	Enabled and up to date

3. Modules that are not installed will state **Not installed (Available online)** in blue text, as shown in the previous screenshot. Currently installed modules should say **Enabled and up to date** in grey text. Check all of the modules for their status before proceeding. If any module is out of date, its status will say **Online upgrade available** in red text. Any out-of-date modules should be upgraded prior to proceeding with the installation of new modules.

> Upgrading all of the modules prior to installing new modules is important. New modules often depend on modules that are already installed. An older version of a dependency may cause unpredictable or broken functionality.

4. As long as all of the modules are up to date, we can start installing new modules. Click on the name of the module that you wish to install.

    Common installation scenarios include:

    -   Office PBX
        -   Voicemail
        -   Day Night Mode
        -   Follow Me
        -   IVR
        -   Music on Hold
        -   Queues

- ○ Ring Groups
- ○ Recordings
- ○ Time Conditions

- • End User Services
  - ○ Voicemail
  - ○ Conferences
  - ○ DISA
  - ○ Info Services
  - ○ VoiceMail Blasting

- • Call Router
  - ○ Blacklist
  - ○ IVR
  - ○ Phonebook Directory
  - ○ Misc Destinations

5. On the **Action** tab, select **Download and Install** as shown in the following screenshot:

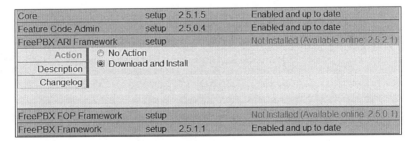

6. Click on the **Process** button in the top right corner of the page. Just like the module update process, we are prompted to confirm the actions that are about to take place:

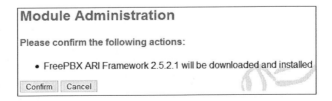

7. Click on the **Confirm** button to start the installation process.

8. Confirmation will be displayed on screen in an orange-colored overlay. Click on the **Return** link to return to the module administration screen.

9. As with any module updates, configuration settings should be applied using the orange-colored **Apply Configuration Changes** bar at the top of the FreePBX interface once, after any new module installations.

If desired, it is possible to install all of the available modules in a single process by clicking on the **Download all** link on the online repository page, and then clicking on the **Process** button. Be aware that this will install every available module, many of which are not needed for most PBX installations.

Installing and updating modules from a file

Nearly, every available FreePBX module can be installed from the online repository. However, there are a few modules that are either from third-party providers that have not yet been accepted into the repository, or have not been updated and have, therefore, been removed from the repository for the current version of FreePBX. Modules such as these can still be installed manually from a file.

Any module that is installed from a file will overwrite any existing module with the same name without warning. Before installing a module from a file, be sure to check that the module is not available from the online repository, and that the module is not already installed.

Installing modules from a file can be dangerous

It can be dangerous to install modules from a file. In most cases, there is a reason why the module is not included in the online repository. Install modules from a file only if they are obtained from a trusted source and are compatible with the version of FreePBX that is currently installed. Because FreePBX inserts code directly into the Asterisk dialplan, a rogue module could open holes into an Asterisk system that could cause very serious financial repercussions.

For example, a module could create a new SIP or IAX2 user account designed to be used by scammers. It is common for scammers to use a hijacked VoIP system to place calls to pay-per-minute telephone numbers that they own. These numbers can charge more than ten dollars per minute. As the provider has no way of verifying who actually placed the call, the owner of the PBX is responsible for all of the charges. Charges in a scam like this can exceed tens of thousands of dollars.

1. The first step in installing a module from a file is to obtain the module. Modules are usually downloadable from the author's web site. Modules should be a single TAR GZIP (`.tgz` or `.tar.gz`) file. This file should be downloaded onto the computer that is being used to administer FreePBX.

2. Once the file has been downloaded, browse to the FreePBX interface and click on the **Module Admin** link in the menu on the left.

3. From the **Module Administration** page, click on the **Upload module** link. An upload form will be displayed as follows:

4. Click on the **Browse** button as shown in the previous screenshot, and locate the module that is to be installed.

5. Click on the **Upload** button as shown in the previous screenshot, and the module will be uploaded to the server and installed. Any errors will be displayed on screen.

6. Once installed, the module will show up on the main module administration screen. Remember to apply configuration changes using the orange-colored **Apply Configuration Changes** bar at the top of the FreePBX interface after installing a new module from a file.

Summary

By now, we should be masters of the FreePBX module universe. We should be able to install, update, and remove modules whenever necessary. A decent starting point (beyond the core modules discussed at the beginning of this chapter) is usually to install the following modules:

- Voicemail
- Follow Me
- IVR
- Queues
- Ring Groups
- Time Conditions
- Music on Hold

These modules will allow basic functionality to be configured. They are also used throughout the rest of the chapters in this book; therefore, installing them is a good idea. A list containing all of the modules can be found in Appendix A, *FreePBX Modules*.

The next chapter will discuss configuring extensions and voicemail boxes.

3
Devices and Extensions

Much like traditional PBX systems, FreePBX uses extensions to route calls to individual users. Each person utilizing the PBX will typically be assigned a single extension. Users can dial an extension to other users directly. Extensions can have voicemail boxes associated with them. They can be members of either ring groups or call queues, or can be targets for direct inbound calls.

Rather than having an extension associated with a particular telephone, FreePBX separates the actual telephones into a concept called *devices*. An extension may be mapped directly to a device in the traditional style, or a device may be independent of an extension and the extension that rings the phone may change based on who is using it. FreePBX supports both of these methodologies.

In this chapter, we will discuss:

- Operational modes for extensions
- Endpoint types
- Common fields
- Setting up a new extension in Extensions mode
- Setting up a new extension in DeviceAndUser mode
- Voicemail setup

Operational modes for extensions

FreePBX has the following two different modes that can be used in order to configure extensions:

- Extensions
- DeviceAndUser

In the **Extensions** mode, each numerical extension that is configured within FreePBX corresponds to a physical telephony endpoint. An endpoint could be a physical telephone, a softphone, an **Analog Telephony Adapter (ATA)**, a speaker, or anything else that talks to Asterisk. In this mode, each endpoint is statically assigned to a particular device. This device never changes.

An example of this would be a typical cubical-office environment. Each cubical has a phone and the extension that rings the phone will never change. Even if the employee who works in a particular cubical is replaced, the extension that rings their phone will remain the same. Most end users find this setup intuitive, as it allows them to dial one number and their call to ring one phone. This mode is the easiest to set up, but offers less flexibility than the DeviceAndUser mode.

In the **DeviceAndUser** mode, the endpoints (devices) and extensions (users) are separated out, allowing one numerical extension to correspond to an unlimited number of endpoints. The DeviceAndUser mode also allows a user to roam from endpoint to endpoint, logging in or out of a phone as their location changes.

An example of this might be a warehouse in which a manager needs to receive calls even while he's on the floor. The manager can select any cordless phone, log into it, and begin his rounds. Any calls to his extension will ring the cordless phone. When he has finished, he logs out of the phone and it no longer rings when his extension is called. This mode can be unintuitive to end users as dialing a person's direct extension number can result in several different phones ringing. This mode is very powerful, but it can be somewhat complicated to set up.

Each operational mode has its own strengths and drawbacks. As with most complex systems, there are multiple ways to accomplish almost any task with FreePBX and Asterisk, so ultimately the mode that you choose should be the one that seems to best suit your environment.

Operational modes can be changed any time, but doing so may mean that a significant amount of reconfiguration is required before the system is fully functional again. It is recommended that an operational mode be chosen prior to configuring any extensions in FreePBX.

The following table lists some common scenarios that may assist in deciding upon the two operational modes for extensions:

Scenario	Operational mode to use
A large business where new employees assume the extension of a person who has left the company. Employees always work at the same telephone.	Extensions
A small business where employees generally work at the same desk, but may opt to work from home. Employees should be able to make and receive calls from home.	DeviceAndUser
A hotel where each room has a static extension associated with it. Regardless of who occupies the room, calling the room's extension will always ring the phone in the room.	Extensions
An executive office where users sit down at a desk on a first come, first serve basis. The phone on their desk needs to ring the extension that is assigned to the person.	DeviceAndUser
A technical support call center where the phone at each station is only used for inbound calls. Employees are not assigned to a particular station, but selected randomly when they report to work.	Extensions
A marketing company where the call center is staffed 24 hours per day. Calls are outbound only, but it needs to track who made which calls. Employees are assigned an extension, and they log into their phone when they start their shift.	DeviceAndUser

Choose extension numbers wisely

No matter which type of operational mode you choose, you must choose extension numbers. It is important to choose extension numbers carefully. Several extension numbers are in use by default in FreePBX (including 70-79, 200, 300-399, 666, 700-799, and 7777). Other extensions are very common and often used as initial weak points for malicious users attempting to gain access to your PBX. It is recommended that you use four-digit extensions if possible, and extensions between 201 and 299 should generally be avoided (the 200 range of extensions is the most common range, and therefore the most targeted). A safe, common practice is to assign the last four digits of a DID as a user's extension number (for example, a DID of 555-555-5432 would ring the user at the 5432 extension).

Endpoint types

FreePBX allows four different types of endpoints to be configured:

- **Session Initiation Protocol (SIP)**
- **Inter-Asterisk eXchange 2 (IAX2)**
- **Zap** (DAHDI)
- Other (custom)

FreePBX does not require a single type to be chosen for all of the endpoints; types can be mixed and matched. As long as the endpoint can communicate with Asterisk using one of these protocols, Asterisk will bridge calls between the devices.

SIP endpoints

SIP endpoints are the most common type of endpoints. Most VoIP hardphones are SIP-based devices. Nearly all of the softphone endpoints support SIP. Choosing to utilize SIP endpoints provides the widest endpoint selection. However, due to the large range of ports required for the **Real-time Transport Protocol (RTP)** audio stream, SIP can be problematic when traversing firewalls and other NAT devices. Common SIP configurations require 10,000 open ports to function correctly. Configuration can be particularly troublesome if both the endpoint and the FreePBX system are behind their own firewalls.

IAX2 endpoints

The IAX2 protocol was designed with the shortcomings of SIP in mind and is most commonly used to link Asterisk systems together. Several endpoints that support IAX2 are on the market, including several softphones and a few hardphones. IAX2 uses a single port for call signaling and transmission of a VoIP audio stream. The choice of IAX2 endpoints can be very limiting, but additional firewall configuration is usually very simple (and often not required at all).

Zap (DAHDI) endpoints

Zap (DAHDI) devices are adapter cards for traditional two-wire **Plain Old Telephone Service (POTS)** handsets (the same handsets that would be found in a home using the traditional telephone service). These cards vary from country to country as telephony standards differ. The cards are installed into a standard PCI or PCI Express slot on a PBX system. Zap (DAHDI) endpoints are the most common adapter cards for analog **Public Switched Telephone Network (PSTN)** telephone handsets.

Zap (DAHDI) cards for PSTN can provide either **Foreign eXchange Station (FXS)** or **Foreign eXchange Office (FXO)** ports. FXS ports are used for connecting analog handsets, while FXO ports are used for connecting analog trunk lines. If Zap (DAHDI) endpoints are being configured, an interface card with FXS ports must be installed.

 Zap is short for Zaptel, an open hardware driver API that was developed to interface analog telephony equipment with digital computer equipment. Due to trademark violations, the Zaptel protocol has been renamed to the DAHDI protocol. The FreePBX interface still references Zap devices as of version 2.5, but it will be updated soon to reflect the change to DAHDI.

Custom endpoints

Custom endpoints can be based on any protocol supported by Asterisk. Custom endpoints are commonly based on the **Media Gateway Control Protocol (MGCP)** and the H.323 protocol. As long as Asterisk can communicate with the endpoint using the Dial command, FreePBX will allow it to be used within its interface.

Common fields

Several common configuration fields exist under both Extensions and DeviceAndUser modes. Regardless of the operational mode that is chosen for FreePBX to operate in, these fields function in the same way. Use this section as a reference when setting up either operational mode. All of the common configuration fields and their purposes are listed here.

Common general Extension/user fields

User Extension should be a unique numerical value. If an extension that is already in use is entered, FreePBX will display a warning when we attempt to save the used extension, and the extension will not be saved. The User Extension number can be dialed from other endpoints attached to the PBX to call this user. This field is required.

Display Name is generally the end user's name or the location of the device (for example, "Alex Robar" or "Server Room"). This value will be displayed as the caller ID text for any calls placed from this user or device to other users or devices on the PBX. This field is required.

CID Num Alias will change the caller ID text displayed when this user calls other users on the PBX. This is commonly used when a user is part of a department in which callbacks should be directed to the department rather than directly to the user (such as a technical support department). This field is not required. If it is left blank, the user's extension will be used to set the **Outbound Caller ID** text.

SIP Alias is used to provide a friendly name for direct SIP calls made to this user. SIP aliases are most often used to distribute an address for contacting a particular user (similar to how email addresses are distributed to allow a user to be sent a message directly).

A SIP alias will allow external callers to dial `alias@example.com` to call this particular user directly, without knowing that user's extension. Note that the SIP Alias field is shown for all types of extensions (SIP, IAX2, Zap, and Custom). Calls to a SIP alias must come from a SIP device, but Asterisk will bridge the call to any type of endpoint that it is able to communicate with. This field is not required. If it is left blank, the only way to place a direct SIP call to the user will be the SIP URL `(extension)@example.com`, where (the extension) is replaced by the user's numerical extension.

Outbound CID is used to set the caller ID text for calls to a number of devices outside of the PBX. This option always requires a digital trunk (PRI/BRI, or VoIP) and setting the caller ID must be supported by the trunk service provider. This field is not required. If it is left blank, the default caller ID name for the trunk placing the call will be used to set the caller ID name text.

Ring Time is the number of seconds to ring the endpoint before dropping the caller to the user's voicemail. FreePBX allows an endpoint to ring between 1 and 120 seconds. If no voicemail is configured for the user, this option will be ignored and the endpoint will ring until the caller hangs up. This field is a dropdown. If it is left at the default value, the extension will ring for the number of seconds configured in the **Ringtime Default** field on FreePBX's **General Settings** page.

Call Waiting enables or disables the call waiting option on a user's extension by default. With call waiting enabled, if a user is called while their endpoint is already in use, the user will be notified of the new incoming call and will be given the option to answer it. Disabling call waiting will send incoming calls to voicemail if the user's endpoint is already in use. Users are able to enable or disable call waiting from their endpoint by dialing a feature code (*70 to activate, *71 to deactivate). This option is simply the initial setting for call waiting on the user's extension. If the call waiting state is toggled from the user's endpoint, then it will stay that way. It will not be overwritten by FreePBX on reloads. This field is a drop-down menu.

Call Screening allows users to hear who is calling before picking up a call. With this option enabled, callers will be prompted to say their name before ringing the user's endpoint. Upon answering the call, the user will hear the caller's name being played back to them and will be given the option to accept or reject the call. Rejected calls are sent to the user's voicemail if configured, or disconnected otherwise. Call screening can either be enabled with memory (caller ID text is remembered, and callers who have identified themselves in the past will never be prompted to do so again unless a fresh copy of Asterisk is installed), or without memory (callers are prompted to identify themselves every time they call in). This field is a dropdown.

The **Assigned DID/CID** group of options allow specific external telephone numbers to be assigned directly to a user's extension. Multiple DIDs can be assigned to a single extension.

DID Description is a description of the number associated with the extension.

Add Inbound DID is the actual number associated with the extension. The number must be in the format that the trunk provider sends it in (often 11 digits or full international dialing standard). **Add Inbound CID** allows only specific caller ID texts on the entered DID to be routed to the user's extension. Caller ID text can be a specific phone number as well as "Private", "Blocked", "Unknown", "Restricted", "Anonymous", or "Unavailable". None of the fields in the Assigned DID/CID group of options are required. If they are left blank, the extension will function as normal, and will only receive calls when an inbound route directs calls to it or another extension calls it directly.

The **Language Code** field will force all of the prompts specific to the user to be played in the specified language (as long as the language is installed and voice prompts for the specified language exist on the PBX). This field is not required. If left blank, prompts will be played back in the default language of the Asterisk server.

The **Recording Options** group of fields allows a user to record incoming or outgoing calls. The user can either dial a feature code (*1) to selectively enable recording for the current call, never record calls, or always record calls. Both the Recording Options fields are dropdowns.

The **Dictation Service** field allows the user to dial a feature code (*34) from their endpoint and have whatever they say recorded. Dictations will be saved in the format selected in the field, and will be emailed to the address specified in the **Email Address** field. Completed dictations are only emailed to the user when they dial the appropriate feature code (*35). Both the **Dictation Service** and **Dictation Format** fields are drop-down menus. The Email Address field is not required. If it is left blank, dictations cannot be emailed to the user once the user has finished recording.

Voicemail & Directory options are discussed in the *Voicemail setup* section of this chapter.

Common endpoint fields

Regardless of the endpoint technology selected, the Emergency CID will be present. The value entered here will override any other caller ID text set for the extension when the user places a call through a route configured for emergency calls in FreePBX. This option is useful for allowing outbound calls to send accurate caller ID text to emergency service dispatch centers, where caller ID text would otherwise provide different information (call centers often provide corporate call back numbers in caller ID text that are assigned to buildings in different physical locations from the call centers themselves). This is especially important for VoIP trunks, as calls over VoIP can originate from anywhere in the world, and the trunks do not carry the information related to location that T1 or PSTN lines do. The Emergency CID field is not required. If it is left blank, the default caller ID settings on a trunk will be used to set the caller ID when an emergency call is placed.

Common SIP/IAX2 fields

SIP and IAX2 endpoints will have a **secret** field. This field has the password that the endpoint will use to authenticate with Asterisk. This field is required.

Choose endpoint passwords carefully

Endpoint passwords are often the weakest link on any externally accessible VoIP system, as malicious users will often attempt to locate extensions having weak passwords. Endpoints that authenticate with Asterisk using passwords such as "1234" stand a good chance of being compromised, allowing an attacker to place calls through your PBX. Pick strong passwords carefully, and ensure that endpoint passwords are not distributed to anyone who does not need to know them.

SIP endpoints will also have a **dtmfmode** field. The DTMF mode for a SIP device specifies how touch tones will be transmitted to the other side of the call. Possible values for this field are **rfc2833, inband, info**, and **auto.** The default value of **rfc2833** is typically fine and should not be changed unless a trunk provider specifically requires it.

It is important to set the DTMF mode correctly based on the trunk. DTMF tones transmitted "inband" on a compressed stream (anything that is not using the ULAW or ALAW codec) will be garbled and will not be recognized on the receiving side. The value rfc2833 will send the tones as data within the RTP payload, and info will send the tones as data in the SIP info headers. Both data methods are more reliable at transmitting understandable tones than inband, but must be supported by the device generating the tones. The **auto** option will attempt to use rfc2833, but will fail over to inband if the receiving host does not indicate support for the data-based tones. The dtmfmode field is required.

Additional SIP fields

Once saved, clicking on a SIP device will show 16 additional options that were not available during the initial setup:

Device Options	
This device uses sip technology.	
secret	my_endpoint_secret
dtmfmode	rfc2833
canreinvite	no
context	from-internal
host	dynamic
type	friend
nat	yes
port	5060
qualify	yes
callgroup	
pickupgroup	
disallow	
allow	
dial	SIP/2223
accountcode	
mailbox	2223@device
deny	0.0.0.0/0.0.0.0
permit	0.0.0.0/0.0.0.0

The **canreinvite** option specifies whether a SIP endpoint can issue re-invites to other endpoints. By default, the media stream for a SIP call will pass through the Asterisk server before reaching the other endpoint, even if both endpoints are on the same network. Re-invites allow two SIP endpoints to take Asterisk out of the media path and speak directly with one another. This can improve latency in certain situations, but for most setups, this will cause dropped calls or unusable call quality. Valid values for canreinvite are **yes** and **no**. This field is not required. If it is left blank, the default value of no will be used.

The **context** option allows the device to be placed into a specific context within Asterisk. A context should have been manually created in the /etc/asterisk/ extensions_custom.conf file for this to work properly. Additionally, the FreePBX **from-internal** context includes all necessary contexts to provide access to all extension features such as voicemail, outbound routes, and feature codes. Specifying a custom context may cause certain FreePBX features to function incorrectly. This field is required.

The **host** option is used to define where calls for an extension should be sent. Valid values are "dynamic", or a specific IP address. Dynamic extensions will register with Asterisk and Asterisk will keep track of where they registered from, hence it knows where to send the call. Endpoints that have dynamic IP addresses should leave this set as "dynamic". Endpoints with static IP addresses can have their IP address entered in this field. These devices are not required to register with Asterisk because when Asterisk receives a call for them, it will forward the call to the configured IP. This field is not required. If it is left blank, the default value of "dynamic" will be used.

The **type** option is used to configure what types of calls will be expected from this extension. Valid options for the type field are **peer**, **user**, and **friend**. From the perspective of the Asterisk server, calls are sent to peer endpoints, they are received from user endpoints, and can be either sent to or received from "friend" endpoints. A normal office telephone handset will be configured as a "friend" endpoint. A call center that does not allow its agents to make outbound calls may configure all of its endpoints as peer endpoints. A hotel lobby may have a phone that is for outbound calls only (to other hotel guests), which would be configured as a user endpoint. This field is not required. If it is left blank, the default value of "friend" will be used.

The **nat** option specifies whether this endpoint is expected to be placed behind a device performing **Network Address Translation** (**NAT**). This option should only be disabled if a specific setup requires internal IP addresses to be sent to a remote Asterisk server (for example, a phone that connects to Asterisk over a VPN and the VPN passes through a NAT device). Valid nat values are **yes** and **no**. This field is not required. If it is left blank, the default value of "yes" will be used.

The **port** option allows a custom port to be set for the endpoint, SIP control data is sent on this custom port. Note that this port is only used for SIP signaling and not for the actual media stream. The default port is **5060**, and most SIP servers will be listening on this port. This option is commonly changed where endpoints are using a connection on which port 5060 is blocked. Note that if the port value is changed, the Asterisk server must also be listening for SIP signaling connections on the custom port specified. Valid values for **port** are numeric entries between 1 and 65,000. This field is not required. If it is left blank, the default value of 5060 will be used.

The **qualify** option will keep track of an endpoint causing Asterisk to ensure that the endpoint is still online. If qualification for an endpoint is enabled, Asterisk will also track its response time relative to the PBX. This option can be useful for tracking latency between the PBX and its endpoints. Running the command `sip show peers` from the **Asterisk command line interface (Asterisk CLI)** will show a list of all SIP endpoints along with the number of milliseconds it has been since the endpoint responded to a qualify request. Valid values for the **qualify** option are **no**, **yes**, or a numerical time value in milliseconds. Setting this option as yes will qualify an endpoint every 200 milliseconds. This field is not required. If it is left blank, the default value of no will be used.

The **callgroup** and **pickupgroup** options allow users to pick up calls that are not directed to them by dialing a feature code (*8). Both values are numeric and range between 0 and 63. Extensions can be placed into multiple groups by separating numerical values by commas. Calls directed to any phone in a particular call group can be answered by any user who is a member of the corresponding pickup group (for example, a user in pickupgroup 1 will be able to pick up any call directed to any phone in callgroup 1). This can be useful for small office or home setups, where it is easier to simply pick up a call from another phone rather than forward that call to another extension. Note that a user can be part of a pickupgroup without being a member of the associated callgroup (for example, a senior staff member may be able to pick up any call directed to anyone in his department, but his department should not be able to pick up calls directed to the senior staff member). Neither the callgroup field nor the pickupgroup field is required. If they are left blank, the endpoint will simply not be a member of a callgroup or pickupgroup, and will not be able to use the call pickup functionality.

The **disallow** option should contain a list of codecs, which the endpoint should not use to communicate with Asterisk. Multiple codecs can be specified separated by spaces. Valid **codec** values are "all", "g723", "gsm", "ulaw", "alaw", "g726", "adpcm", "slin", "lpc10", "g729", "speex", and "libc". It is common practice to first disallow all codecs in this line, and then, specifically allow a select few using the **allow** option. This field is not required. If it is left blank, no codecs will be disallowed, and Asterisk may attempt any codec available to it when establishing a call to the endpoint.

The **allow** option is the opposite of the **disallow** option, and is used to specify which codecs should be used for communication with the endpoint. Codecs are used with preference to the order in which they are specified. The allow option has the same valid values as the disallow option. This field is not required. If it is left blank, no codec will be preferred by the endpoint, and Asterisk may use any codec available to it when establishing a call to the endpoint. Asterisk will give preference to codecs that do not require transcoding.

Transcoding

The codecs that each side of a call supports play the biggest role when choosing a default codec for an endpoint or a trunk. The rule of thumb for codec selection is to try and configure an endpoint to use the same codec as the trunk it will be using for external calls. When an endpoint uses a different codec than the trunk carrying the endpoint's call, Asterisk must convert the call's audio stream on the fly. This process is known as **transcoding**. Transcoding uses processor resources and can bog down an Asterisk server. A system performing transcoding for every call is able to handle a significantly fewer number of concurrent calls than a system that does not.

Transcoding also incurs a latency penalty for the call's audio (that is, the time between when one party says something and the other party hears it is increased). Depending on the original quality of the call before transcoding, this could be enough to make an audible difference in the amount of lag time that each party on the call hears. In extreme cases, it may not be possible to carry on a conversation. Zap/DAHDI trunks (PSTN lines, PRI lines, and T1 lines) will use the G.711 codec. North American and Japanese style trunks should use the G.711 ULAW codec. Trunks in other areas of the world should use G.711 ALAW. VoIP trunks will typically use either G.711 or G.729 and they may support both.

Transcoding costs can be determined by running the command `show translation` at the Asterisk CLI. Asterisk will output a matrix of all the codecs it can use and the latency penalty that a call will incur when being transcoded between each available codec. The matrix looks similar to the one shown as follows:

```
       g723 gsm ulaw alaw g726 adpcm slin lpc10 g729 speex ilbc
 g723   -    -    -    -    -    -     -    -     -    -     -
  gsm   -    -    2    2    2    2     1    3     -    -     27
 ulaw   -    5    -    1    2    2     1    3     -    -     27
 alaw   -    5    1    -    2    2     1    3     -    -     27
 g726   -    5    2    2    -    2     1    3     -    -     27
adpcm   -    5    2    2    2    -     1    3     -    -     27
 slin   -    4    1    1    1    1     -    2     -    -     26
lpc10   -    5    2    2    2    2     1    -     -    -     27
 g729   -    -    -    -    -    -     -    -     -    -     -
speex   -    -    -    -    -    -     -    -     -    -     -
 ilbc   -    6    3    3    3    3     2    4     -    -     -
```

Note that certain codecs may need to be purchased (for example, Digium sells the G.729 codec on a per-channel basis). Some codecs may be free, but will need to be installed before they can be used, such as Speex.

The other factor to consider during codec selection is the available bandwidth where the Asterisk server resides.

The G.711 codecs (`ulaw` and `alaw`) use about 64 kbps for each side of the call (that is, 64 kbps for sending what is said, and 64 kbps for receiving what the other party says, for a total of 128 kbps). The G.729 codec knocks the required bandwidth down to 8 kbps for each side of the call. The iLBC can use about 15 kbps per side of the call, and Speex is a variable bit-rate codec, using between 4 kbps and 48 kbps for each side of the call. Using 128 kbps of bandwidth to connect a phone over a local network to Asterisk is certainly no problem as there will be plenty of bandwidth to spare. Although, when VoIP trunks or phones outside of the local network come into play, bandwidth is significantly limited. Many broadband providers have a limited upload speed of 768 kbps or less (this is especially common for DSL connections). Factoring in normal connection overhead, this leaves us with space for about 10 active calls if we use G.711, but dozens of calls if we use G.729.

The rule of thumb when selecting a codec is to try to use the same codec for endpoints and trunks as long as the bandwidth required for doing so does not exceed available resources. If matching the codecs is not possible, the next best method is simply to balance the requirement for lowering bandwidth against the requirement for reducing transcoding as much as possible. Keep in mind that not all of the endpoints must use the same codec. For example, if all calls go out of G.711 trunks, it is always feasible to have all of the endpoints on the network that is local to Asterisk use G.711, while endpoints outside of the network (that connect to Asterisk over a broadband connection) use G.729. This method will only use transcoding for those endpoints that are outside of the office. External calls will use 16kbps of bandwidth to connect with Asterisk.

The **dial** option is the dial string Asterisk will use to call the endpoint. Any valid Asterisk dial string is admissible for this option. This field is required.

The **accountcode** option is typically used for billing purposes. A string value of length up to 20 characters may be used for the account code. The value entered here will show up in the Asterisk CDR for every call placed by this extension. This field is not required. If it is left blank, the CDR will log the extension that placed a call, but will not log any account code associated with the call.

The **mailbox** option is used to specify the voicemail box that the device will be checking. The SIP protocol will return the number of waiting messages in the specified mailbox when this device queries Asterisk for waiting messages. Most endpoints will provide some kind of indication when their mailboxes have messages in them (such as a flashing light or a stuttering dial tone). Valid values are any mailboxes that have been created using FreePBX or entered manually into the `/etc/asterisk/voicemail.conf` file. This field is not required. If left blank, the endpoint will not check to see if any voicemail messages are waiting.

The **deny** option specifies network addresses from which Asterisk should not accept traffic for this peer. This option should be in the format of an IP address and subnet, such as 192.168.1.0/255.255.255.0 (to disallow traffic for this extension from the IP range of 192.168.1.1 to 192.168.1.254). It is possible to enter a value of 0.0.0.0/0.0.0.0 to deny all of the networks by default, and, to enter specific networks from which traffic can be accepted in the **permit** option. This option is commonly used to restrict endpoint usage to a particular network, so that if the endpoint is stolen or otherwise removed from the network, it cannot be used to place calls and will be essentially useless. This field is not required. If it is left blank, Asterisk will not block traffic for this peer from any IP address.

The **permit** option is the opposite of the **deny** option. Specific IP addresses or networks can be added in this option to allow traffic for this extension from the entered IP/network. This field is not required. If it is left blank, traffic will be allowed from all IP addresses.

Additional IAX2 fields

Once saved, clicking on an IAX2 device will show 13 additional options that were not available during initial setup:

Device Options

This device uses iax2 technology.

secret	my_endpoint_secret
notransfer	yes
context	from-internal
host	dynamic
type	friend
port	4569
qualify	yes
disallow	
allow	
dial	IAX2/2224
accountcode	
mailbox	2224@device
deny	0.0.0.0/0.0.0.0
permit	0.0.0.0/0.0.0.0

The additional options shown for IAX2 endpoints are very similar to the additional options shown for SIP endpoints. The only additional option available to IAX2 endpoints is the **notransfer** option. The IAX2 notransfer option is the equivalent of the SIP canreinvite option (although the values are reversed). Setting the notransfer option to **yes** prohibits the media path from being transferred away from Asterisk, keeping Asterisk in the media path at all times. If notransfer is set to **no**, IAX2 endpoints will be able to communicate directly with one another, removing Asterisk from the media path entirely.

All other additional IAX2 options are equivalent in functionality to their SIP option counterparts.

Common Zap fields

Zap endpoints will have a **channel** field. It refers to the Zap channel that the Asterisk Zaptel (DAHDI) driver will use to communicate with the Zap endpoint. The channel is specific to each type of Zap card. Running the `ztcfg` command from the Linux command line will output a list of all Zaptel (DAHDI) devices on the system and a list of how many channels each device has. The value that is entered into the channel field must be present in the list that the `ztcfg` command returns.

Additional Zap fields

Once saved, clicking on a Zap device will show 14 additional options seen in the following screenshot, which were not available during initial setup:

Device Options	
This device uses zap technology.	
channel	zap/g1
context	from-internal
immediate	no
signalling	fxo_ks
echocancel	yes
echocancelwhenbridged	no
echotraining	800
busydetect	no
busycount	7
callprogress	no
dial	ZAP/zap/g1
accountcode	
callgroup	
pickupgroup	
mailbox	2225@device

Several additional Zap configuration options are equivalent to their SIP or IAX2 configuration option counterparts.

The **immediate** option will cause Asterisk to start executing its dialplan for this extension as soon as the handset goes "off hook", without the caller ever having to dial anything. This option is commonly used for emergency phones, such as phones in an elevator, so that the emergency personnel are contacted as soon as someone picks up the phone. This option is useful only if a custom context has been built to support it, and that context is specified in the context option. Custom contexts must be manually written into the /etc/asterisk/extensions_custom.conf file.

The **signalling** option is used to specify the type of signaling used by the channel. Only one type of signaling can be used per Zap endpoint. Signaling is specified using a string, and could be any one of almost 40 possible values. Most Zap handset endpoints will use FXS_KS (Foreign eXchange Station-Kewl Start). Check with the device manufacturer to determine which signaling type the endpoint uses.

The **echocancel** option enables *software* echo cancellation for the endpoint. This is not to be confused with hardware echo cancellation that some devices have as an option. Hardware echo cancellation must be configured on the device itself. The echocancel option can be set to one of these values—**no, yes, 16, 32, 64, 128,** or **256**. Setting the option to "no" disables echo cancellation. Setting the option to "yes" enables echo cancellation with a value of 128. The numerical value specified in the echocancel option is the number of taps that Asterisk will use to sample the media stream to determine the best way to cancel an echo on the call. One tap is one sample from the data stream. Note that if this option is set to anything other than one of the valid values specified, Asterisk will default the option to yes (128 taps) without warning. It is recommended to leave echo cancellation enabled for all of the devices that do not have hardware echo cancellation built into them. If hardware echo cancellation is present, the **echocancel** field should be set to "no".

The **echocancelwhenbridged** option allows echo cancellation to be enabled or disabled for calls that are bridged between two Zap devices. As most of the time the calls between two Zap endpoints will not have any echo, this option is not required. It is best practice to begin adjusting for echo only after the echo is experienced, rather than trying to adjust the echo cancellation properties based on echoes that might occur. Valid values for the echocancelwhenbridged field are **yes** or **no**.

The **echotraining** option allows a Zap channel to train itself for the proper echo cancellation requirements for the call, before the call begins. Valid values for echo training are "yes", or they may be numbers between 10 and 4,000. When enabled, Asterisk will mute the channel at the beginning of any call made to or from this device for the number of milliseconds entered as a value. During this time, a pulse will be sent to the other side of the call, and the information gathered from whatever echo of this pulse is returned, which will be used to fine tune the echo cancellers on the channel. This can often result in echo-free calls from the very beginning of the conversation, instead of forcing the echo trainer to begin training after the call has already started. As with the echowhenbridged field, it is a good idea to start adjusting the echotraining field only after the echo is experienced.

The **busydetect** option is used to detect if a called Zap channel returns a busy tone. As Zap endpoints are typically analog devices and can therefore not return their status to Asterisk, enabling the busydetect option allows Asterisk to know that the called endpoint is in use and enables calls to be routed appropriately based on that information. Valid values for this option are "yes" and "no".

The **busycount** option works in conjunction with the busydetect option. If the busydetect option is set to "yes", the value set in the busycount option is used as the number of busy tones for which Asterisk will wait before it determines that a channel is busy. Valid values are whole numbers greater than 1. The higher this value is, the longer a busy channel will take to disconnect. However, lower values may cause repetitive sounds in a conversation to be treated as busy/disconnect tones, and that call will be terminated. The default value of **7** is recommended.

When enabled, the **callprogress** option will force Asterisk to try to recognize various analog tones, which are types of **Special Information Tone (SIT)**, in order to determine how a call is progressing. Asterisk will attempt to recognize ringing tones, busy tones, disconnection tones, or sounds indicating that a call has been answered. Although this option typically provides few benefits, it will usually result in quicker termination of disconnected channels.

Common custom fields

Custom endpoints will have a **dial** field. This field is for specifying a custom `Dial` command that Asterisk will use to communicate with the endpoint (using a protocol that is not SIP, IAX2, or Zap). Common custom dial strings are `H323/${EXTEN}@(IPADDRESS)` for an H.323 device, and `MGCP/${EXTEN}@(IPADDRESS)` for an MGCP device. The `IPADDRESS` token should be replaced with the IP address of the device being added.

Setting up a new extension in Extensions mode

In Extensions mode, each user who is defined in FreePBX has a single endpoint associated with them. Extensions mode is a good choice for simple setups where each person configured on the PBX is always expected to be using the same phone. If your FreePBX system is configured in the DeviceAndUser mode, you can skip this section.

Configuring FreePBX for Extensions mode

Switching FreePBX between operational modes is done from the console by editing, the /etc/amportal.conf file.

> If FreePBX was configured to use Extensions mode during initial installation, no additional configuration is required to begin creating extensions. These instructions only need to be followed if FreePBX was set up to use the DeviceAndUser mode during the initial installation.

Log in to the console as the root user and open the amportal.conf file for editing using the following command:

```
nano /etc/amportal.conf
```

Look for the line that starts with AMPEXTENSIONS=. This line can be quickly located by pressing *Ctrl + W* to load the nano command's search feature, typing in AMPEXTENSIONS, and pressing the *Enter* key. Once the line is located, change this line to read AMPEXTENSIONS=extensions.

Press *Ctrl + O* to save the changes to the amportal.conf file. Press *Ctrl + X* to exit the text editor.

Now that the configuration file has been updated to run FreePBX in Extensions mode, run the following to force FreePBX to pick up the changes:

```
/usr/src/freepbx-2.5.1/apply_conf.sh
```

FreePBX will now be running in Extensions mode, and you can log out of the console.

Configuring extensions

Now that FreePBX is running in Extensions mode, we can begin creating extensions. Each endpoint used will require a unique extension. To configure extensions, navigate to the FreePBX interface and click on the **Setup** tab in the navigation bar on the left as shown in the following screenshot:

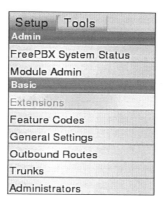

Click on the **Extensions** link under the **Basic** header. The **Add an Extension** screen will be displayed:

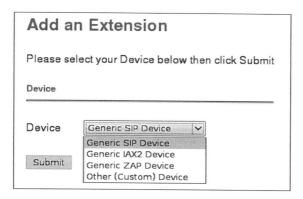

From the **Device** drop-down menu, select the type of endpoint that is being configured (SIP, IAX2, Zap, or other). Click on the **Submit** button. Additional form fields will be displayed like those in the following screenshot:

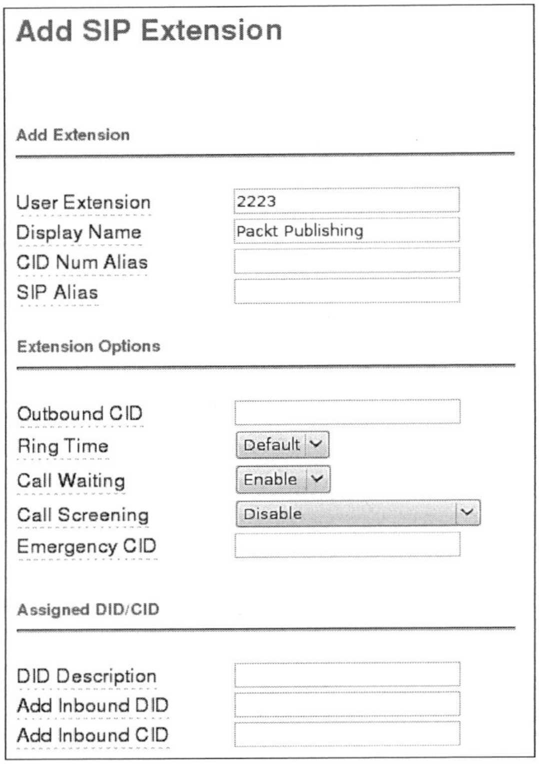

Add SIP Extension

Add Extension

User Extension	2223
Display Name	Packt Publishing
CID Num Alias	
SIP Alias	

Extension Options

Outbound CID	
Ring Time	Default ▾
Call Waiting	Enable ▾
Call Screening	Disable ▾
Emergency CID	

Assigned DID/CID

DID Description	
Add Inbound DID	
Add Inbound CID	

Fill out the form fields with the appropriate information. Information on most fields can be found in the *Common fields* section covered earlier in this chapter. Information regarding the **Voicemail & Directory** group of fields can be found in the *Voicemail setup* section of this chapter. Information regarding the **VmX Locater** group of fields can be found in the *Follow Me and the VmX Locater* section of Chapter 7, *Call Routing*.

Note that only **User Extension, Display Name,** and if present, **secret** are required fields. All other fields can be left at their default values and the extension will still be created successfully. In addition, all fields except for the User Extension field can be altered after the extension has been saved.

A list of all of the user extensions that already exist is present on the right side of the screen. This list can be used to easily determine the next available unique extension number.

Once all fields have been filled out, click on the **Submit** button at the bottom of the page to save the extension:

The extension that was just saved will be in the extension list on the right side of the screen as shown in the following screenshot:

Before the extension can be used, the configuration changes must be applied to FreePBX. Click on the orange-colored **Apply Configuration Changes** bar at the top of the screen:

Once a device is saved, clicking on the device name in the active extensions list will provide additional options that were not accessible during the extensions initial setup for SIP, IAX2, and Zap devices.

 Custom devices do not have any additional options.

FreePBX assigns the most common values to these additional options. Typical setups will not require any changes.

Setting up a new extension in DeviceAndUser mode

In the DeviceAndUser mode, each user defined in FreePBX can have multiple endpoints associated with them. DeviceAndUser mode is a good choice for more complex setups, where each person configured on the PBX is expected to work from multiple, different phones or multiple locations. If your FreePBX system is configured in the Extensions mode, this section can be skipped.

Configuring FreePBX for DeviceAndUser mode

Switching FreePBX between operational modes is done from the console by editing the /etc/amportal.conf file.

> If FreePBX was configured to use DeviceAndUser mode during initial installation, no additional configuration is required to begin creating devices and users. These instructions only need to be followed if FreePBX was set up to use the Extensions mode during initial installation.

Log in to the console as the root user, and then open amportal.conf for editing:

```
nano /etc/amportal.conf
```

Look for the line that starts with AMPEXTENSIONS=. This line can be quickly located by pushing *Ctrl + W* to load the nano command's search feature, typing in AMPEXTENSIONS, and pressing the *Enter* key. Once this line is located, change it to read AMPEXTENSIONS=deviceanduser.

Press *Ctrl + O* to save the changes to the amportal.conf file. Press *Ctrl + X* to exit the text editor.

Now that the configuration file has been updated to run FreePBX in DeviceAndUser mode, run the following to force FreePBX to pick up the changes:

```
/usr/src/freepbx-2.5.1/apply_conf.sh
```

FreePBX will now be running in DeviceAndUser mode, and you can log out of the console.

Configuring users

Now that FreePBX is running in DeviceAndUser mode, we can begin creating users on the system. Each user will require a unique numerical extension. To configure users, navigate to the FreePBX interface and click on the **Setup** tab in the navigation bar on the left.

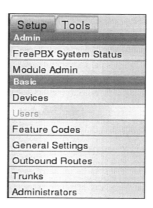

Click on the **Users** link under the **Basic** header. The **Add User/Extension** screen will be displayed:

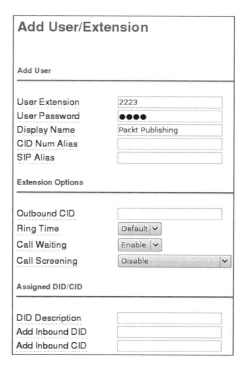

Fill out the form fields with the appropriate information. Besides the common configuration fields, there will be a **User Password** field. This field is a numerical password that this user can use to log into any endpoint attached to the PBX.

Information on most fields can be found in the *Common fields* section earlier in this chapter. Information regarding the **Voicemail & Directory** group of fields can be found in the *Voicemail setup* section later in this chapter. Information regarding the **VmX Locater** group of fields can be found in the *Follow Me and the VmX Locater* section of Chapter 7.

Note that only **User Extension, User Password,** and **Display Name** are required fields. All of the other fields can be left at default values and the extension will still be created successfully. In addition, all fields except for the User Extension field can be altered after the extension has been saved.

> A list of all of the user extensions that already exist is present on the right side of the screen. This list can be used to easily determine the next available unique extension number.

Once all of the fields have been filled out, click on the **Submit** button at the bottom of the page to save the extension:

The user that was just saved will now be shown in the active user list on the right side of the screen:

Before the extension can be used, the configuration changes must be applied to FreePBX. Click on the orange-colored **Apply Configuration Changes** bar at the top of the screen as shown in the following screenshot:

Once a user is saved, clicking on the user name in the active users list will load the user settings to be edited. Certain modules such as **Follow Me** and Gabcast will add additional options that were not accessible during the user's initial setup to this page:

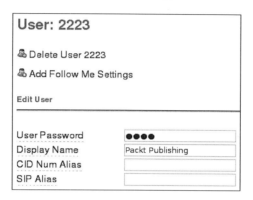

Follow Me Settings are discussed in Chapter 7. Once a user is configured, we can proceed with configuring devices.

Configuring devices

With a user configured, it is now possible to configure devices. To configure devices, navigate to the FreePBX interface and click on the **Setup** tab in the navigation bar on the left in the following screenshot:

Click on the **Devices** link under the **Basic** header. The **Add Device** screen will be displayed:

From the **Device** drop-down menu, select the type of endpoint that is being configured (SIP, IAX2, Zap, or other). Click on the **Submit** button. Additional form fields will be displayed like those in the following screenshot:

Fill in the appropriate form fields on this screen. The form fields on this screen vary depending on the type of endpoint that will be in use. All endpoint types will have fields for **Device ID, Description, Emergency CID, Device Type,** and **Default User**.

The Device ID field is a unique numerical value that is used by Asterisk to dial the device. SIP and IAX2 devices will require this value when the devices themselves are being configured.

> A list of all of the devices that already exist is present on the right side of the screen. This list can be used to easily determine the next available unique device ID number.

Description is a text description of the purpose of the device. It is common to use this field to describe the location of the device or its MAC address.

The Device Type field can be either "fixed" or "adhoc". A **fixed** device will always have the same user logged into it (it will not be possible for the user to log out of the device). An **adhoc** device allows users to log in and out of itself at will. When a user is logged into an ad-hoc endpoint, any calls to their extension will ring that endpoint. Users can be simultaneously logged into as many endpoints as they wish.

The user selected in the Default User dropdown is the user that will be logged into the device by default. Fixed devices require this value to be set. Adhoc devices can have this value set to "none" so that no user is logged into the device by default.

Once all of the required form fields are filled, click on the **Submit** button at the bottom of the page to save the device, as shown in the next screenshot:

Device Info	
Device ID	102223
Description	Front Desk SIP Hardphone
Emergency CID	
Device Type	Fixed
Default User	2223

Submit

FreePBX® Freedom to Connect®

FreePBX is a registered trademark of Atengo, LLC.
FreePBX 2.5.0 is licensed under GPL

Once a device is saved, clicking on the device name in the active devices list will load additional device configuration options that were not available during the initial setup for SIP, IAX2, and Zap devices.

 Custom devices do not have any additional options.

FreePBX assigns the most common values to these additional options. Typical setups will not require any changes.

Voicemail setup

The voicemail capabilities built into Asterisk compare well against enterprise-level voicemail solutions. FreePBX makes voicemail boxes a breeze to set up.

Voicemail delivery options

Voicemail options are located either on the **Extensions** page (if FreePBX is operating in Extensions mode), or on the **Users** page (if FreePBX is operating in DeviceAndUser mode). From the FreePBX navigation menu, either click on **Extensions** or on **Users**, click on the name of the user for whom we will be configuring the voicemail settings in the active users list, and scroll to the bottom of the page to view voicemail settings:

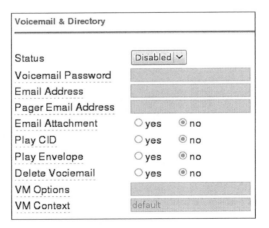

The **Status** field can be set to either "Enabled" or "Disabled". If voicemail is disabled, messages cannot be left for the user and calls directed to them will continue to ring until the caller hangs up. All other voicemail options are disabled, unless this field is set to "Enabled".

The **Voicemail Password** field should be set to a numerical password that the user will enter to access their message center. This setting can also be changed by the user from their VoIP endpoint.

If a valid email address is entered in the **Email Address** field, any time a voicemail is left for the user an email message will be sent to the address entered here. By default, the message will simply notify the user that a new message has been left for them. Only one address can be entered into this field.

The **Pager Email Address** field can be used to have Asterisk send a short message to a mobile device whenever a new message is left in the user's voicemail. The message will be under 140 characters, and is typically used in conjunction with SMS or pager mobile services. Note that this field is *not* for a mobile phone number, but rather an email address that will reach a mobile device. Most mobile carriers provide an email-to-SMS gateway service that can be used to send emails to mobile telephones. Only one address can be entered into this field.

If the **Email Attachment** field is set to **yes**, the email message sent to the address in the Email Address field will have a copy of the voicemail attached to it. This message can then be played through the speakers of the computer on which it was received. Messages are not attached to email notifications sent to the address in the Pager Email Address field.

If the **Play CID** field is set to **yes**, the system will play back the caller ID number of the person who left the message prior to the message being played.

If the **Play Envelope** field is set to **yes**, the user will hear the date and time that the message was left prior to hearing the message being played.

If **Delete Voicemail** field is set to **yes**, new messages will be deleted from the user's messaging center as soon as the notification email is delivered to the address specified in the Email Address field. Be very careful with this option, because FreePBX will allow you to delete the message without having a copy of it attached to the email notification. This could mean that a message is left and a notification email is sent to the user, but the actual voicemail that was left will not be accessible at all.

The **VM Options** field can contain any option that would normally be specified in the /etc/asterisk/voicemail.conf file. These options can enable other options such as forcing a user to record their name and greeting before listening to messages, increasing the volume on voicemail messages as they are recorded, or enabling a warning for the user if they are using a temporary greeting as their outgoing message. Details on these options can be found in Appendix C, *Voicemail. conf Options*, or in the Asterisk documentation for the voicemail.conf file. Multiple options can be entered into this field by separating the options with commas.

The **Voicemail Context** field is a string value that can be set to any valid context configured within the /etc/asterisk/voicemail.conf file. Voicemail contexts can be used to apply one collection of settings to a particular group of mailboxes. If you have not manually edited the voicemail.conf file to create your own voicemail contexts, leave it as "default".

When configuring voicemail settings is complete, click on the **Submit** button at the bottom of the page followed by the orange-colored **Apply Configuration Changes** bar at the top of the page.

Managing voicemail messages

There are two primary ways for a user to manage their voicemail messages:

- The Asterisk messaging center
- The Asterisk Recording Interface web site built into FreePBX

Users can dial *97 to access their own mailbox when dialing from their own extension (Extensions mode), or from the device where their extension is logged in. They will be prompted for a password only. If the user is calling from someone else's phone on the PBX, they can dial *98. They will be prompted for their extension and their password. Once a valid password has been entered, the user will hear voice prompts that direct which buttons to press on their touch tone telephone or softphone in order to listen to and manage their voicemail messages.

Once logged into the messaging center, the following options are valid:

- 1: Plays the oldest unheard message (if any), or plays the oldest message that is still stored. When listening to a message, the following options are valid:
    - 3: Advanced options (allows the user to send a voice reply, call back the caller ID who left them a message, and hear date and time information about the voicemail)
    - 4: Play the previous message
    - 5: Repeat the current message from the beginning
    - 6: Play the next message
    - 7: Delete the current message
    - 8: Forward the message to another user on the PBX
    - 9: Save the message to another folder
    - *: Rewind the message five seconds
    - #: Fast forward the message five seconds

- 2: Change folders
- 3: Advanced mailbox options
- 0: Mailbox options. Once in mailbox options, the following options are valid:
  - ○ 1: Record unavailable message
  - ○ 2: Record busy message
  - ○ 3: Record name
  - ○ 4: Change voicemail password
  - ○ *: Return to the main menu

If the user would like to have a visual overview of their messages, voicemail messages can be administered from the **Asterisk Recording Interface (ARI)** web site that is built into FreePBX. To access ARI, visit the IP address of your FreePBX server in the recordings directory (for example, `http://192.168.0.10/recordings`). The ARI login screen will be shown:

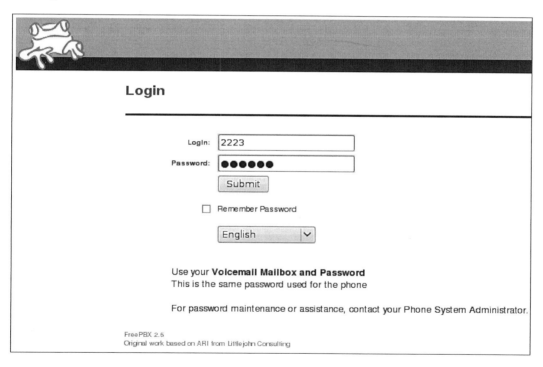

Users can log in to ARI using their extension number for the **Login** field and their voicemail password for the **Password** field. Once logged in, users will see a visual representation of their voicemail messages:

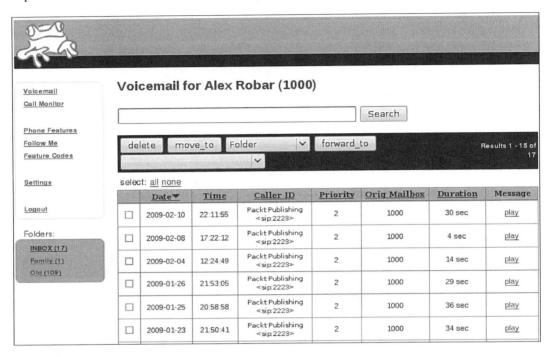

From the ARI main screen, users will be able to play messages by clicking on the **play** link in the **Message** column.

A message can be deleted by clicking on the checkbox next to the message date and clicking on the **delete** button.

A message can be moved into another folder by clicking on the checkbox next to the message date, selecting a new folder in the **Folder** dropdown, and then clicking on the **move_to** button.

A message can be forwarded to another user by clicking on the checkbox next to the message date, selecting a user in the empty second-row dropdown, and then clicking on the **forward_to** button.

Directory listing

Most PBX systems allow a caller to press the pound (#) key to search through a directory of all users who are configured on the PBX, by last name. FreePBX supports listing users by first name, last name, or both in the directory. The only configuration step required to have a user listed in the directory is to enable voicemail for them. As soon as voicemail is enabled for a user, that user becomes listed in the directory. A user cannot be listed in the directory without having voicemail enabled for their account.

To configure directory options, click on the **General Settings** link in the FreePBX navigation menu:

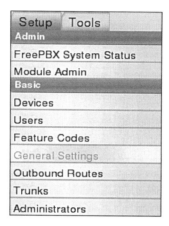

Company directory options can be found midway down the page:

Company Directory	
Find users in the Company Directory by:	first or last name ⌄
Announce Extension:	☑
Operator Extension:	2223

There are very few company directory options. The **Find users in the Company Directory by** option can be set to "first name", "last name", or "first or last name". Users who are listed in the directory can be searched by whatever name this option specifies.

If enabled, the **Announce Extension** option will play the extension that the caller is being transferred to when the caller locates the person they are looking for in the directory. If this option is disabled, the caller is simply transferred to the extension without any additional messages.

The **Operator Extension** is the number that a caller will be transferred to if they press *0* while in the directory. This option can be an extension, ring group, queue, or even an external telephone number.

Summary

In this chapter, we learned how to create users and endpoints in either Extensions or DeviceAndUser mode. We also discussed the distinctions between devices and users when FreePBX is run in the DeviceAndUser mode. After this chapter, we should have a FreePBX system configured with user accounts and device options that are appropriate for our network. We also learned how to create a voicemail box for each user, and how to manage voicemail boxes using both the Asterisk messaging center and the ARI web site. Each user account on our PBX should now have a voicemail box and be listed in the directory.

In the next chapter, we will learn how to connect our PBX with the outside world or other PBX servers using trunks.

4
Trunks

A trunk in the simplest of terms is a pathway into or out of a telephone system. A trunk connects a PBX to outside resources, such as PSTN telephone lines, or additional PBX systems to perform inter-system transfers. Trunks can be physical, such as a PRI or PSTN line, or they can be virtual by routing calls to another endpoint using **Internet Protocol (IP)** links. In this chapter, we will discuss the following:

- Various types of trunks allowed by FreePBX
- Methods for setting up each type of trunk
- Checking the status of any configured trunk

Trunk types

FreePBX allows the creation of six different types of trunks as follows:

1. Zap
2. IAX2
3. SIP
4. ENUM
5. DUNDi
6. Custom

Zap, IAX2, and SIP trunks utilize the technologies of their namesake. These trunks have the same highlights and pitfalls that extensions and devices using the same technology do. Zap trunks require physical hardware cards for incoming lines to plug into. SIP trunks are the most widely adopted and compatible, but have difficulties traversing firewalls. IAX2 trunks are able to traverse most firewalls easily, but are limited to adoption mainly on Asterisk-based systems.

In terms of VoIP, **ENUM (E.164 NUmber Mapping)** is a method for unifying E.164 (the international telecommunication numbering plan) with VoIP routing. The ENUM system can be considered very similar to the way that the Internet DNS system works. In the DNS system, when a domain name is looked up an IP address is returned. The IP address allows a PC to traverse the Internet and find the server that belongs to that IP address. The ENUM system provides VoIP routes back when queried for a phone number. The route that is returned is usually a SIP or IAX2 route.

An ENUM trunk allows FreePBX to send the dialed phone number to the public e164.org ENUM server. If the called party has listed their phone number in the e164.org directory, a VoIP route will be returned and the call will be connected using that route. A VoIP route contains the VoIP protocol, the server name or IP address, the port, and the extension to use in order to contact the dialed phone number. For example, a SIP route for dialing the number 555-555-1234 might appear as SIP:1234@pbx.example.com:5060. This is advantageous in several ways. It is important to note that indirect routes to another telephony system are often costly. Calling a PSTN telephone number typically requires that call to route through a third-party provider's phone lines and switching equipment (a service they will happily charge for). If a number is listed in the ENUM directory, the returned route will bridge the call directly to the called party (or their provider), bypassing the cost of routing through a third party.

ENUM also benefits the called party, allowing them to redirect inbound calls to wherever they would like. Service disruptions that would otherwise render a particular phone number useless can be bypassed by directing the phone number to a different VoIP route in the ENUM system.

More information on ENUM can be found at the following web sites:

- The ENUM home page: http://www.enum.org/
- The e164.org home page: http://www.e164.org/
- The Internet Engineering Task Force ENUM charter:
  http://www.ietf.org/html.charters/enum-charter.html

DUNDi (Distributed Universal Number Discovery) is a routing protocol technology similar to ENUM. In order to query another Asterisk system using DUNDi, that system must be "peered" with your own Asterisk system. Peering requires generating and exchanging key files with the other peer.

DUNDi is a decentralized way of accomplishing ENUM-style lookups. By peering with one system you are effectively peering with any other system that your peer is connected to. If system A peers with system B, and system B peers with system C, then system C will be able to see the routes provided by system A. In peer-to-peer fashion, system B will simply pass the request along to system A, even though system C has no direct connection to system A.

DUNDi is not limited to E.164 numbering schemes like ENUM and it allows a PBX to advertise individual extensions, or route patterns, instead of whole phone numbers. Therefore, it is a good candidate for distributed office setups, where a central PBX can be peered with several satellite PBX systems. The extensions on each system will be able to call one another directly without having to statically set up routes on each individual PBX.

More information on DUNDi can be found at the following web sites:

- DUNDi home page: `http://www.dundi.com/`
- Example DUNDi SIP configuration: `http://www.voip-info.org/wiki/view/DUNDi+Enterprise+Configuration+SIP`
- Example DUNDi IAX2 configuration: `http://dundiglobal.org/documentation/tying-two-pbxs-together-using-dundi-and-iax2`

Custom trunks work in the same fashion as custom extensions do. Any valid Asterisk `Dial` command can be used as a custom trunk by FreePBX. Custom trunks typically use additional VoIP protocols such as H.323 and MGCP.

Setting up a new trunk

Setting up a trunk in FreePBX is very similar to setting up an extension. All of the trunks share eight common setup fields, followed by fields that are specific to the technology that trunk will be using.

Trunk configurations for common VoIP providers are listed in Appendix D, *Common Trunk Configurations*.

In order to begin setting up a trunk, click on **Trunks** in the left side navigation menu as shown in the following screenshot:

From the **Add a Trunk** screen, click on the name of the technology that the trunk will be using (for example, if a SIP trunk will be used, click on **Add SIP Trunk**) as shown in the following screenshot:

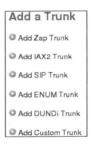

Common trunk setup fields

No matter which technology a trunk will be using, the same eight fields will appear first on the configuration page as shown in the following screenshot:

Outbound Caller ID sets the caller ID name and number that will be displayed to the called party. Caller ID should be in the format of "Name" <##########>, where "Name" is the name that will be displayed, and <##########> will be the telephone number displayed. Be sure to include the quotes and angle brackets to send both name and number information. In order to send just a telephone number without a name, simply put the telephone number in the **Outbound Caller ID** field without quotes or angle brackets. Note that setting outbound caller ID only works on digital lines (T1/E1/J1/PRI/BRI/SIP/IAX2), not POTS lines. The ability to set outbound caller ID must also be supported by your provider.

> FreePBX will ignore the **Outbound Caller ID** field if it is not in the proper format. Be sure that a caller ID with a name and number contains a name in quotes and a telephone number in angle brackets. A caller ID with just a telephone number must only contain the number and nothing else. FreePBX will not set the caller ID on outbound calls that do not match one of these two formats.

The **Never Override CallerID** checkbox should be selected in order to disable any other part of FreePBX from setting the caller ID on this trunk. If this box is checked, a caller ID value must be set in the **Outbound Caller ID** field. This option is useful when the trunk connects with a provider who will drop calls that set a different caller ID than the one they are expecting. This can often mean that calls that are forwarded out to an external number ("hair-pinning" a call) will be dropped, as FreePBX will attempt to set the caller ID to that of the original caller. If inbound calls are routed back through this trunk and the provider seems to be dropping them, try turning this option on.

Maximum Channels is the maximum number of *outbound* calls that this trunk can support. Note that FreePBX does not count inbound calls against the channel limit. Whole numbers greater than one are the only valid values for this field. If no limit should be imposed, leave this field blank.

The **Disable Trunk** checkbox allows a trunk to be temporarily disabled in any outbound route where the trunk is in use. If a trunk is experiencing difficulties, it can be disabled here in order to have outbound calls skip the trunk entirely in their routing sequence. Under normal circumstances, a downed trunk will simply refuse a call, but in scenarios in which a trunk accepts a call but fails to connect it properly, this option is especially useful. Without disabling the trunk in this scenario, all of the calls will be dropped. Disabling the trunk allows outbound calls to bypass the problematic trunk while it is repaired, instead of having to remove the trunk entirely and recreate it when the problem is resolved.

The **Monitor Trunk Failures** field allows an AGI script to be called when a trunk fails. FreePBX determines that a trunk has failed when calls cannot be completed and the returned status from Asterisk is *not* BUSY, NOANSWER, or CANCEL. Scripts specified in this field can perform any action that can be scripted, including reloading Asterisk configuration to force trunk re-registration, or notifying a system administrator of the failure through email. Failure scripts must be located in the /var/lib/asterisk/ agi-bin directory. The full name of the failure script should be specified.

Dial Rules allow dialed numbers to be manipulated before they are passed to the trunk. Dialed numbers are altered based on the patterns entered into this field. There should only be one pattern per line. Only the first matched rule will be acted upon (other patterns will be ignored, even if they match). Patterns are matched based upon the order they are listed in, that is, from top to bottom. Patterns can consist of the following items:

Pattern	Description
X	Any whole number from 0-9
Y	Any whole number from 1-9
N	Any whole number from 2-9
[#]	Any whole number or letter in brackets. Note that multiple numbers can be separated by commas, and a range of numbers can be specified with a dash ([1,3,6-8] would match the numbers 1, 3, 6, 7, and 8).
.	Matches one or more characters (acts as a wildcard)
|	Removes a prefix from the dialed number (555|1234567 would take 5551234567 and pass 1234567 to the trunk)
+	Adds a prefix to the dialed number (555+1234567 would take 1234567 and pass 5551234567 to the trunk)

Note that wildcards are not valid before a "+" or "|". Also, "+" and "|" can be used in the same pattern (0|01+15551234567 would take 015551234567 and pass 0115551234567 to the trunk). Dial rules are very useful for allowing users to continue dialing numbers the way they are accustomed to, even if the provider is expecting them to be delivered in a different way.

A few real-world examples of dial pattern usage are given below:

Scenario	Dial Pattern(s)
Users are used to dialing 9 to access an outside line. A FreePBX system replaces their existing PBX, but should accommodate this dialing pattern instead of forcing users to learn a new one. The provider is expecting all of the numbers to be sent in standard North American 10 digit format.	9|1+NXXNXXXXXX 9|1NXXNXXXXXX
The provider requires an account code to be sent in front of all of the dialed calls (in this example, the account code is 654321). Calls must be sent in standard North American 10 digit format.	5432101+NXXNXXXXXX 543210+1NXXNXXXXXX
The provider requires all of the numbers to be sent in standard North American 10 digit format except for toll free calls. Toll free calls should never send the leading 1.	1|888NXXXXXX 1|866|NXXXXXX
In this example, note the order that items are listed in. If the last item were listed first and a user were to dial *800-555-1234*, a 1 would be appended and sent to the provider, and the call would fail.	1|877|NXXXXXX 1|800|NXXXXXX 1+NXXNXXXXXX

Dial Rules Wizards are pre-constructed dial patterns for use in the **Dial Rules** field. Selecting the name of one of the pre-made patterns will populate the **Dial Rules** box with the appropriate pattern.

Outbound Dial Prefix can be used in order to add a prefix to every single call dialed through this trunk. This option can be useful if accessing an outside line requires dialing an extra number (usually 9). This option can also be useful for certain Zap cards that are slow to pick up the line and therefore, start dialing before the line is listening for the digits. Adding a "w" as the outbound dial prefix will cause the system to wait for 50 milliseconds before dialing (multiple "w" characters can be strung together to create a longer wait). Anything that is valid in an Asterisk dial string command can be entered into this field.

Zap trunks

Beyond the common trunk fields, Zap trunks only have one additional field to fill in as shown in the following screenshot:

Zap Identifier (trunk name) should match the group (and optionally the channel number) that is set up for this Zap trunk in the `/etc/asterisk/zapata.conf` file. `Zapata.conf` will have a section like the ones below for each Zaptel card that is present in the system:

```
context=from-zaptel
group=0
signalling = fxs_ks
channel => 1
context=from-zaptel
group=0
signalling = fxs_ks
channel => 2
```

Entering a value of **g0** in the **Zap Identifier (trunk name)** field will call each channel in group zero sequentially until it finds one that picks up. Alternatively, it is possible to separate out each channel in unique trunks by entering values such as *g0-1* for group zero, channel one, *g0-2* for group zero, channel two, and so on.

When all of the required values have been entered, click on the **Submit** button to write the changes to the database. As with all of the changes, click the orange-colored **Apply Configuration Changes** bar to load the new configuration changes into memory.

IAX2 and SIP trunks

IAX2 and SIP trunks share the same additional configuration settings as shown in the following screenshot:

Trunk Name is a "friendly" name. This value is not parsed by FreePBX in any way; it is simply used to refer to the trunk in other parts of the FreePBX interface.

PEER Details are the outbound configuration details that would normally be placed into `iax.conf` or `sip.conf` for IAX2 or SIP trunks, respectively. These details will vary widely from trunk to trunk, and should be supplied by the trunk provider. By default, FreePBX populates this field with the most commonly required values.

In the **PEER Details** field, **host** is the IP address or DNS hostname of the provider. This is the destination server or network that Asterisk will send calls to when they use this trunk. The **username** and **secret** lines are for the credentials used to authenticate this trunk against the provider. The **type** line should almost always be set to **peer**, as this designates that this set of details is for a destination that Asterisk is sending calls to (not receiving calls from).

The **USER Context** field is the telephone number, account number, or account name that your provider is sending inbound calls to. Some providers will simply send a call to the registered IP address, in which case this field is not required.

The **USER Details** field is for the inbound configuration details that would normally be placed into the `iax.conf` or `sip.conf` files for IAX2 or SIP trunks, respectively. As with the **PEER Details** field, these details can vary widely, but will likely be supplied by the trunk provider.

In the **USER Details** field, the **secret** line is the **password** that the provider will use to authenticate incoming calls against. The **type** line should almost always be set to **user**, as this designates that this set of details is for a peer that Asterisk is receiving calls from (not sending calls to). The **context** line indicates the context that inbound calls from this trunk should be sent to. Unless you have defined custom contexts, leave this field set to **from-trunk** to allow FreePBX to process the calls.

Order is important

The order that parameters are specified in for both the **PEER Details** and **USER Details** fields is important. Details are set from top to bottom. If a certain parameter appears twice in one of these fields, the second instance of it will be used and the first will be ignored. If *allow=ulaw* is followed by *deny=all*, all of the codecs will be denied and the allow statement will be ignored. Pay close attention to how these parameters are ordered. It can often save hours of troubleshooting later on when a trunk seems to be refusing calls for no reason at all.

The **Register String** is also a setting that should be supplied by the trunk provider. The value in this field will cause FreePBX to attempt to register with the trunk provider. Registration lets the provider know where to send calls when they come in for your telephone number. The register string is usually in the format of [username]:[password]@[voipserver] (for example, 5551234567:password@sip.example1.com). If a register string is not provided then the provider must be set up in order to send calls to a specific IP address, and the IP address of your VoIP server must not change.

ENUM trunks

ENUM trunks require absolutely no additional configuration beyond the common configuration fields. The only item worth noting for ENUM trunks is that all of the calls are queried against the e164.org database. e164.org expects calls to be in the format of [CountryCode][PhoneNumber], so adjust dial patterns appropriately for your location.

DUNDi trunks

DUNDi trunks require a bit of prep work before they can be successfully used to route calls. Before a DUNDi trunk can be set up, your PBX must be peered with one or more nodes. Peering DUNDi nodes are not set up within the FreePBX interface. Peering is completed by editing the /etc/asterisk/dundi.conf file on both PBX systems.

Once the PBX systems have been peered, FreePBX can be used to create a DUNDi trunk. Beyond the common fields, DUNDi trunks only require one additional piece of information as shown in the following screenshot:

The **DUNDi Mapping** field tells FreePBX which DUNDi context to query for results. It is possible to have various DUNDi contexts for sharing different types of VoIP routes. One might have one DUNDi context for sharing local extensions between branch offices, and another context for advertising which external phone numbers they own. Each DUNDi context will require its own DUNDi trunk within FreePBX.

To find the name of the DUNDi context, open the `/etc/asterisk/dundi.conf` file for editing, and look for the `[mappings]` section. The section should look like the following:

```
[mappings]
priv => dundi-localextensions,0,IAX,priv:${SECRET}@pbx.examplehost.
com/${NUMBER},nopartial
pub => dundi-publicnumbers,0,IAX,priv:${SECRET}@pbx.examplehost.com/
${NUMBER},nopartial
```

In this example, `priv` is the name of the DUNDi context that advertises local extensions. Asterisk will advertise any extension that exists under the `dundi-localextensions` dialplan context if a peer queries it using this context. Likewise, `pub` is the public DUNDi context that will advertise any telephone route listed in the `dundi-publicnumbers` dialplan context. Type the name of the DUNDi context that this trunk will query into the **DUNDi Mapping** field and click on the **Submit** button. Once the changes have been saved, click on the orange-colored **Apply Configuration Changes** bar at the top of the screen.

Custom trunks

Custom trunks are very similar to custom extensions and devices. There is only one additional field for setting up custom trunks as shown in the following screenshot:

The **Custom Dial String** can be any valid dial command that would normally be used in the Asterisk dialplan, with one notable exception: the called number is inserted into the dial string using the `$OUTNUM$` variable. For example, the string to call an H.323 device at IP address 192.168.1.2 might be `H323/192.168.1.2/$OUTNUM$`.

As with any changes made to FreePBX, make sure to click on the **Submit Changes** button, followed by the orange-colored **Apply Configuration Changes** bar at the top of the screen to save and reload all of the settings.

Checking trunk status

Trunk status can either be checked manually using various Asterisk CLI commands, or FreePBX can monitor the health of all of the trunks automatically and run a script when there is a failure.

Checking trunk status using the Asterisk CLI

Checking trunk status using the Asterisk CLI can be done from within FreePBX using the Asterisk CLI module. In order to access the CLI module, click on the **Tools** tab in the navigation menu and then click on the **Asterisk CLI** link under the **System Administration** heading as shown in the following screenshot:

The **Asterisk CLI** page will be shown as follows:

Asterisk CLI

Command:

Execute:

The **Asterisk CLI** page contains a single text box where any command that would normally be typed into the Asterisk CLI can be entered. When the **Execute** button is clicked, the command is run and the results are returned on screen.

 The commands below demonstrate two useful CLI commands for checking trunk status. The CLI can also be used to show extensions, installed codecs, a transcoding matrix between different codecs, and many other useful pieces of information. For a complete listing of CLI commands, please see http://www.voip-info.org/wiki/view/ Asterisk+CLI.

In order to check the status of a SIP trunk, enter the sip show registry command:

```
Host                    Username      Refresh  State
sip.provider1.com:5060   5551234567        120  Request Sent
sip.provider2.com:5060   5550123456        105  Registered
```

The Host column lists the host that the trunk is trying to register with. The Username column is the username supplied for the trunk by the provider. This may be the DID/telephone associated with the trunk, but it does not have to be. Refresh is the number of seconds before the trunk status will be refreshed again. The State column shows the health of the trunk, and should indicate whether or not the trunk is registered.

The State column may list one of the following values:

State	Explanation
Request Sent	A registration request has been sent to the server listed in the Host column, but no response has been received yet. The trunk is not registered at this point, and will not route calls. The Request Sent state does not indicate success or failure, but simply indicates that the trunk is currently attempting to register with the provider.
	It is common to see the Request Sent state immediately after Asterisk has been reloaded, after a period of Internet connectivity disruption, or after the provider has experienced downtime.

State	Explanation
Timeout	Asterisk was unable to register with the provider. Several requests were sent, but none of them received a response from the provider. The trunk is not registered at this point, and will not route calls.
	The Timeout status indicates that there is a connectivity problem. The Internet connection that the PBX uses may be down, or the provider's registration server may be down. Whatever the case may be, Asterisk is not able to contact the server specified in the Host column. As long as the correct server is specified, the trunk will most likely come up on its own once connectivity is restored.
Rejected	The server specified in the Host column was contacted by Asterisk, but rejected the credentials that were provided. The trunk is not registered at this point, and will not route calls.
	Either the **username** or **secret** values need to be adjusted in the trunk's configuration in order to match the credentials provided by the host. Without manual intervention the trunk will most likely never register.
Registered	The trunk is registered. The supplied credentials were authenticated against the server specified in the Host column. The trunk is functional and will route calls.

In the above sip show registry example, there are two SIP trunks set up under FreePBX. The first trunk is attempting to register a username of 5551234567 against a server at sip.provider1.com. The state of Request Sent means that Asterisk has sent a registration request to the provider, but has not yet received a response.

The username of 5550123456 has a state of Registered. This means that the trunk has successfully registered to a SIP server at sip.provider2.com. Calls received by the provider for this trunk will be sent to the PBX.

Checking IAX2 trunk status from the CLI is very similar to how SIP trunks are checked. In order to check the status of the IAX2 trunk, run the iax2 show registry command:

```
Host              Username Perceived            Refresh  State

4.1.1.1:4569      098564   1.1.1.1:4569         60       Registered

4.2.2.2:4569      6840372  <Unregistered>       60       Rejected

4.3.3.3:4569      727044   <Unregistered>       60       Timeout
```

IAX2 trunks show more detailed status information than SIP trunks do. Hostnames are always resolved to their IP addresses instead of listing the hostname in the Host column. The Perceived column shows the IP address that the provider sees your PBX at. The Username, Refresh, and State columns serve the same purpose as they do in the SIP trunk status table.

In this example, username 098564 is successfully registered to 4.1.1.1. The provider sees this trunk as registering from an IP address of 1.1.1.1. The username of 6840372 is attempting to register against an IAX2 server at 4.2.2.2, but the request is being rejected. A state of Rejected indicates that the register string provided in the trunk's FreePBX configuration page is invalid. The username of 727044 is attempting to register with an IAX2 server at 4.3.3.3, but the request timed out. A state of Timeout indicates that the IAX2 server's trunk is attempting to register, but cannot be contacted. The server may be offline or there may be network disruptions preventing VoIP traffic from reaching the server.

Monitoring trunk status with FreePBX failure scripts

Every trunk created with FreePBX has a **Monitor Trunk Failures** field as shown in the following screenshot:

In order to enable this feature, first select the **Enable** checkbox next to the field, and then enter the name of the script that should be executed when the trunk fails. The asterisk user must be able to execute scripts. Scripts must be located in the /var/lib/asterisk/agi-bin directory.

A failure script will only be executed if a trunk does not accept a call for abnormal reasons. Reasons such as "busy signal" (the dialed number is already engaged by another caller), "congestion" (no more available channels on the trunk), or "no answer" (the call continually rings and nothing/nobody answers) are valid reasons for a failed call, and the failure script will not be executed.

Failure scripts do not stop call processing. If a call would normally cycle through three trunks and the first trunk is down, the failure script will execute and the system will proceed to attempt the call on the second and third trunks.

Failure scripts can be used for a variety of purposes. The most common failure script is an alert script that sends an email on failure:

```
#!/bin/bash
EMAIL=admin@examplecompany.com
DATE=`date`
HOST=`hostname`
MESSAGE="A trunk has failed on $HOST at $DATE"
echo -e "$MESSAGE" | mail -s "Trunk Failure" "$EMAIL"
```

This script simply emails the date and the hostname of the Asterisk system to the email address defined in the EMAIL variable.

Another popular failure script is the one that will force Asterisk to reload its configuration, thereby forcing all of the trunks to re-register with their providers:

```bash
#!/bin/bash
EMAIL=admin@examplecompany.com
DATE=`date`
HOST=`hostname`
/usr/sbin/asterisk -rx "reload"
SIPTRUNKS=`/usr/sbin/asterisk -rx "sip show registry"
IAXTRUNKS=`/usr/sbin/asterisk -rx "iax2 show registry"
MESSAGE="A trunk failure forced a reload on $HOST"
MESSAGE="$MESSAGE\nDate: $DATE"
MESSAGE="$MESSAGE\nCurrent Trunk Status:"
MESSAGE="$MESSAGE\n\nSIP Trunks:\n$SIPTRUNKS"
MESSAGE="$MESSAGE\n\nIAX2 Trunks:\n$IAXTRUNKS"
echo -e "$MESSAGE" | mail -s "Trunk Failure" "$EMAIL"
```

This script forces a reload using asterisk -rx "reload", and then gathers trunk status using the show registry commands. All of the gathered data is then emailed to the address specified in the EMAIL variable.

The above scripts are just a few basic samples of the kinds of workflow that can be executed when a trunk fails. Failure scripts can be written in any AGI-compatible language such as Perl, PHP, C, Pascal, BASH, and Java.

Summary

By now we should have a FreePBX system with some fully-functional trunks configured. We should be able to configure a new trunk of any type, and be able to check the status of our trunks using the Asterisk command line interface (Asterisk CLI), if necessary. We should also have a good idea about how to monitor the health of each trunk, and how to alert an administrator on failure.

Now that we have operational trunks, the next chapter will walk through setting up various call targets so that incoming calls coming in through our brand new trunks have something to route to.

5
Basic Call Targets

A call target in FreePBX is any kind of destination for a phone call that enters the system. A target might be a voice-response menu that prompts the caller to press various digits to route their call, a ring group to call a number of endpoints, or virtually any other type of processor to route the call in whatever way is desired. A call may have several targets throughout its lifespan on a PBX.

The following types of call targets are available in FreePBX:

1. Terminate Call
2. Extension
3. Voicemail
4. Ring Groups
5. Conferences
6. Day Night Mode
7. Phonebook Directory
8. Queues
9. Time Conditions
10. IVR (Digital Receptionist)

This chapter will cover the first seven targets (the "basic" call targets) of the above list. The more advanced call targets will be covered in the next chapter. Basic call targets generally have a single, easy-to-configure function, whereas advanced call targets tend to have several functions and are more complicated to configure.

Chapters 5 and 6 deal strictly with understanding and configuring the different types of call targets. These call targets are put to use through the configuration of inbound routes and users' follow-me settings. Once all the required call targets have been configured, please see Chapter 7, *Call Routing* for information on routing inbound calls to the new call targets.

Terminate Call

FreePBX provides several clever ways to terminate calls. We may wish to terminate a call because the calling number is a known telemarketer, or perhaps the caller has attempted to reach an invalid extension too many times. Whichever the case, the following options are available for the **Terminate Call** target:

- **Hangup**: Terminates the call immediately without any further call processing or signaling.

- **Congestion**: Sends a signal indicating that there are no channels available to complete the call before terminating it. This is used only for digital channels (such as SIP, IAX, or PRI). Some providers will use this signal to locate an alternate route or process the call in another way.

- **Busy**: Relays a busy tone to the caller. The call terminates when the calling party hangs up (FreePBX will play a busy tone indefinitely).

- **Play SIT Tone** (Zapateller): Plays a SIT known as an operator intercept to the calling party. An operator intercept tone consists of two short tones and one long tone. It is designed to indicate that the called number is not in service. SIT tones are recognized by a large portion of automated dialing equipment, so this tone is often useful for playback to known telemarketing numbers. Automated dialers who understand this tone will usually remove the called number from their dialing lists. Once the intercept tone is played, the call will be terminated immediately.

- **Put caller on hold forever**: As one might imagine, it places the calling party on hold until they terminate the call themselves.

- **Play ringtones to caller until they hangup**: It continually plays back a ringing tone to the calling party until they terminate the call themselves.

Be aware of indefinite termination options

The **Busy, Put caller on hold forever,** and **Play ringtones to caller until they hangup options** open up the possibility of a call never terminating until the PBX or the calling party loses connectivity and the call is dropped. In most environments, this could possibly mean a call that lasts for weeks. With VoIP providers charging by the minute, such calls can get expensive very quickly.

The latter two options are typically used only to annoy unwanted callers. Indefinite ringtones or hold music are relatively safe for these kinds of calls as the caller will terminate the call themselves when they do not receive a human on the other end of the line. Nevertheless, be aware of the activity on your PBX to avoid the bill for a week-long session of hold music. When in doubt, terminate the call rather than opting to leave it on hold indefinitely. It is always more cost effective to play an SIT tone and then drop the call than it is to leave the call on hold for any period of time.

Extension and Voicemail

The **Extension** target will route calls directly to a particular extension. The only option available for the Extension target is which extension to send a call to. If FreePBX is in Extensions mode, an extension must have been previously created for this target to be available. If FreePBX is in DeviceAndUser mode, a user must have been previously created for this target to be available.

The **Voicemail** target will route calls directly to an extension's voicemail box without ringing the extension first. The Voicemail target provides options of selection such as **busy, unavail,** or **no-msg**. These options control the outgoing message that will be played prior to playing the standard instructional message asking the caller to leave a message. If the selected message does not exist, a standard message stating that the person at the called extension is either on the phone or unavailable will be played. For the voicemail target to be available, the **Voicemail & Directory** option must be enabled when setting up an extension or user.

Ring Groups

A ring group allows one call to ring any number of endpoints. It is typically used for a particular department or section of a building. A company might use a ring group to ring all phones in the sales department. A home might use a ring group to ring all phones on a particular floor. Ring groups must be set up prior to selecting them as a call target. To set up a ring group, click on the **Ring Groups** option under the **Inbound Call Control** header in the FreePBX navigation menu as shown in the next screenshot:

The **Add Ring Group** screen will be displayed as shown in the next screenshot:

Each field or dropdown should be configured to ensure the ring group behaves in the desired manner.

The **Ring-Group Number** is a number that can be dialed from internal endpoints to access this ring group. Users can either dial this number directly, or transfer a caller they have on the line to this number. The Ring-Group Number can be thought of as the extension number of the ring group.

The **Group Description** field is just used to identify this ring group when selecting it as a call target. The contents of this field are not visible to callers in any way.

The **Ring Strategy** dropdown defines the way in which the endpoints in this ring group will be rung. Endpoints can be rung using the following methods:

- **ringall**: Ring all group members listed in the Extension List field at the same time.

- **ringall-prim**: If the first extension listed in the Extension List is not in use, all group members will be rung at the same time. If the first extension is in use or is in the do-not-disturb mode, none of the extensions will be rung and the call will immediately fail over to the target selected in the **Destination if no answer** section.

- **hunt**: Ring each group member one at a time in the order that they are listed in the Extension List field.

- **hunt-prim**: Functions similar to the ringall-prim method. If the first extension is in use, no group members will be rung. Otherwise, each extension is rung in the same fashion as in the hunt method.

- **memoryhunt**: Rings the first extension listed in the Extension List field, then rings the first and second extensions listed in the Extension List field, then rings the first, second, and third extensions listed in the Extension List field (and so on until all extensions are ringing or a timeout is reached).

- **memoryhunt-prim**: If the first extension is in use no group members will be rung. Otherwise, each extension is rung in the same fashion as in the **memoryhunt** method.

- **firstavailable**: Rings the first extension in the Extension List that is available to ring. If an extension has call waiting enabled, it will be considered "available", even if it is already on a call.

- **firstnotonphone**: Rings the first extension in the Extension List that is completely unoccupied. Call waiting settings are not taken into account. If an extension is already on a call, it will not be rung whether or not call waiting is enabled.

The **Ring Time (max 60 sec)** field is for defining the number of seconds that the ring group will be rung before failing over to the **Destination if no answer** field. For the hunt type of strategies, the ring time is applied to each stage of the hunt sequence. For example, if the Ring Time (max 60 sec) field is set to "30" and the Ring Strategy field is set to "memoryhunt", the first extension in the Extension List will be rung for 30 seconds. Following this, the first and second extensions will be rung for 30 seconds, then the first, second, and third extensions will be rung for 30 seconds, and so on until the end of the Extension List is reached.

Extension List contains a list of all extensions to ring. Extensions should be listed one per line. Available internal extensions can also be selected from the **Extension Quick Pick** dropdown to insert them into the Extension List. Any extension listed here will be rung directly and Follow Me Settings will not apply. To force the ring group to respect Follow Me Settings, append the pound (#) symbol to the extension number (for example, 5001#).

External phone numbers or extensions can be added to a ring group by suffixing them with a pound symbol as well (for example, 11234567890# would dial 1-123-456-7890 whenever the ring group is called). As long as a trunk exists to route the number, it will be dialed as part of the ring group. Note that external numbers will take longer to connect, so ring groups that include them are likely to have longer ring times.

The pound symbol is also used to include internal resources that are not extensions to the group. In this fashion, it is possible to ring other ring groups or queues simply by adding their number to the Extension List and suffixing it with a pound.

The message selected in the **Announcement** dropdown will be played to the caller entering the ring group prior to any extensions being rung.

The music on hold category selected in the **Play Music On Hold?** dropdown will be played to the caller while the ring group members are being rung. Selecting the **Ring** option will cause the caller to hear the ringing instead.

The **CID Name Prefix** field will prefix the caller ID of all calls to this ring group with the value specified here. This is useful for the person receiving the call as they can determine if a caller is attempting to call them directly or is calling a larger group.

The **Alert Info** field is used to transmit some information in the ALERT_INFO SIP headers to a SIP endpoint. Some SIP endpoints can be set up to play alternate ringtones depending on the ALERT_INFO data they receive. If the endpoint being rung does not use SIP technology, this field is ignored for that endpoint.

When the **Ignore CF Settings** option is checked, any extension in the Extension List that has call forwarding enabled will not be rung.

When the **Skip Busy Agent** option is checked, any extension in the Extension List that is in use will not be rung. This option will ignore call waiting settings, so multi-line or single-line phones with call waiting enabled will not be rung if they are in use at all.

The **Confirm Calls** option will prompt the person who answers the call to press *1* on their phone before the call is actually bridged to their extension. This is often useful for ring groups that contain external phone numbers in the Extension List. If one of the external phone numbers goes to voicemail, the PBX will see that the call has been "answered" and will bridge the caller to the external number even though a real person did not answer the call. If the call is not confirmed by the external party, the call will continue ringing the rest of the Extension List as normal. The Confirm Calls option will only work with the ringall ring strategy.

The **Remote Announce** and **Too-Late Announce** dropdowns are only applicable if the Confirm Calls option is enabled. The message in the Remote Announce field is played to the person who picks up the call (this should be a message asking them to press *1* to confirm the call). The message in the Too-Late Announce field is played to the person who picks up the call if someone else in the ring group picked up the call before they were able to confirm it. Default messages for these two fields do not exist and must be recorded. More information on recording custom voice prompts can be found in the *Custom Voice Prompts* section of Chapter 9, *Personalizing Your PBX*.

The **Destination if no answer** section is used when nobody in a ring group picks up the call within the designated ring time.

Look at the options in the following screenshot:

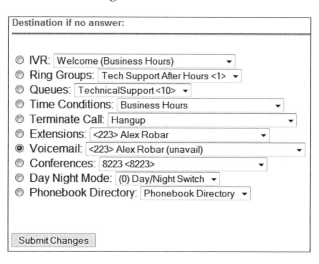

The destination chosen is a normal call target. The options available in this section will vary depending on which type of targets have already been configured in FreePBX.

Once all options have been configured, click on the **Submit Changes** button, followed by the orange-colored **Apply Configuration Changes** bar.

Conferences

Conferences allow two or more calls to be joined together so that all parties on the call can hear one another. At least one conference room must be configured before this target option is available. To configure a conference room, click on the **Conferences** link under the **Internal Options & Configuration** header in the FreePBX navigation menu:

The first section of the **Add Conference** screen requires a number and description for the conference room that is being created:

Add Conference

Add Conference

Conference Number:	
Conference Name:	
User PIN:	
Admin PIN:	

The **Conference Number** is a number that internal endpoints can dial to reach this conference. Like the ring groups, this can be thought of as the extension number of the conference.

The **Conference Name** is meant to identify the purpose of the conference room. The name is used only when selecting the room as a call target, and is not visible by the caller in any way.

The **User PIN** is a numeric passcode that is used to enter the conference room. If a PIN is entered in this field, no one is able to join the conference room without entering the PIN.

The **Admin PIN** functions in the same way as the **User PIN**. The Admin PIN and User PIN should not be set to the same value. The Admin PIN is used in conjunction with the **Leader Wait** option explained further in this chapter, in order to identify the administrator or leader of the conference.

The second section of the Add Conference page sets up general conference options that determine how the conference room behaves when in use:

The **Join Message** option is a message that will be played to anyone attempting to join the conference. The caller will hear this message before their channel is bridged into the conference room.

If the **Leader Wait** option is set to "Yes", the conference will not begin until the conference administrator joins the conference room. The administrator is identified by the Admin PIN option. If other callers join the conference room before the leader does, they will hear on-hold music or silence until the conference begins (what they hear depends on the **Music on Hold** option explained later in this section). If this option is set to "No", the callers will be bridged into the conference as soon as they call the conference room number.

If the **Quiet Mode** option is set to "No", a tone will be played whenever a caller enters or exits the conference room.

If **User Count** option is set to "Yes", the number of users currently in the conference room will be announced to the caller before they are bridged into the conference.

If **User join/leave** option is set to "Yes", the caller will be prompted to say their name and press the pound (#) key before joining the conference. The existing room occupants will hear the name of the new caller being played back before the user is bridged into the conference room.

If the **Music on Hold** option is set to "Yes", on-hold music will be played if there is only one caller in the conference room or the conference has not started yet (because the leader has not arrived). If this option is set to "No", no sound will be played during these situations.

If **Allow Menu** is set to "Yes", conference participants are able to press the asterisk (*) key on their phones to be presented with an audio menu that only they can hear. The menu gives them the ability to mute/unmute their channel, increase/decrease their transmit volume, and increase/decrease their receive volume. If this option is set to **No**, pressing the asterisk key will do nothing. The available menu options and their functions are listed in the following table:

Menu option	Action
1	It toggles mute for the user. When enabled, anything the user says is not transmitted to the rest of conference members. If the conference is being recorded, anything said by a muted user is not part of the recording.
2	It toggles the conference lock. When a conference is locked, no more callers may join. A locked conference must be unlocked for any new users to join. This option is only available to a conference administrator. If the conference does not have an admin PIN configured or the user has joined the conference as a user instead of an admin, this option is not available.
3	It ejects the last user who joined the conference from the conference room. The user will hear a message informing them that they have been ejected from the conference and that their call will be terminated. Note that if a conference is unlocked, the user may rejoin. The best way to remove an abusive conference user is to eject them and then immediately lock the conference. This option is only available to a conference administrator. If the conference does not have an admin PIN configured, or the user has joined the conference as a user instead of as an admin, this option is not available.
4	It decreases receive volume. The user can tap this option to decrease the volume of what they are hearing. This does not affect what any other conference member hears. If a user is finding other conference members too loud, they can press 4 a few times while in the conference menu to make the conference quieter for themselves.

Menu option	Action
5	It increases receive volume. The user can tap this option to increase the volume of what they are hearing. This does not affect what any other conference member hears. If a user is having trouble hearing other members of the conference, they can press *6* a few times while in the conference menu to make the conference louder for themselves.
6	It decreases transmit volume. The user can tap this option to decrease the volume of what they are transmitting to the rest of the conference members. When this option is used, the user will sound quieter to all other conference members. If a user is much louder than the other members of a conference room, they can tap *7* a few times while in the conference menu to make their transmit volume quieter.
7	Increases transmit volume. The user can tap this option to increase the volume of what they are transmitting to the rest of the conference members. When this option is used, the user will sound louder to all other conference members. If the conference members are having trouble hearing a particular user, that user can tap *9* a few times while in the conference menu to make their transmit volume louder.

If the **Record Conference** option is set to **Yes**, all the channels that are bridged together for the conference will be recorded into a single WAV file. The file will be stored in the /var/spool/asterisk/monitor folder, and the filename will have a time and date stamp of when the conference ended.

Day Night Mode

Day Night Mode targets act as simple toggle switches for a call. Each target has two predefined call targets of its own. When a call is routed to a Day Night Mode target, it will be routed to one of these two destinations depending on whether the target is in day mode or night mode. Day Night Mode targets are used to override normal call flows in FreePBX. For example, a company may route calls to their receptionist during business hours and to voicemail after hours. If the company has a half day, this would normally require FreePBX to be reconfigured to route the calls to voicemail. With a Day Night Mode target, one of the employees could dial a special feature code, force the PBX into night mode, and redirect all calls to voicemail for the rest of the day. The default feature code to toggle a Day Night Mode control is *28(index), where (index) is the feature code index assigned to the Day Night Mode control (for example, index 1 would use *281 to toggle the control). Up to ten Day Night Mode targets can exist on a single FreePBX system.

The terms "day" and "night" are often confusing, as the target does not have to be used for day and night operations. Day Night Mode targets are simply logic gates where calls can take one of two paths depending on whether the gate is **on** or **off**.

To configure a **Day Night Mode** target, click on **Day/Night Control** under the **Inbound Call Control** header in the FreePBX navigation menu:

Day Night Mode targets have six options that can be configured as shown in the following screenshot:

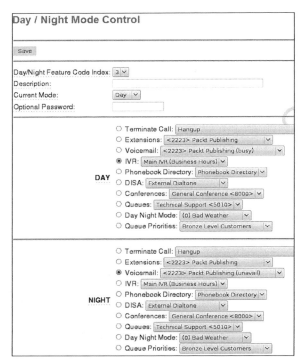

The **Day/Night Feature Code Index** is used to identify the target to the caller who is changing his mode. To change the mode to **Day** or **Night,** a caller will dial the day/night mode feature code (by default *28 on FreePBX) followed by this index code. For example, if index one is in day mode, dialing *281 will toggle the mode of index "1" to night mode. Dialing *281 again will toggle it back to Day mode.

The **Description** field is meant for describing the purpose of this target. This field is used for selecting the target and is not visible to the caller in any way.

The **Current Mode** dropdown shows the current state of the target. Existing targets can have their states changed by altering this field.

The **Optional Password** field provides password protection for the target if desired. This can be useful to protect call flow on a PBX so that only a few key individuals can override it if necessary and no one is able to accidentally disrupt normal operations. The password should be a numeric value. If a Day Night Mode target has a password associated with it, the user will be prompted for the password after they dial the appropriate feature code toggle. Only after the user enters the correct password will the mode of the Day Night Mode target be toggled.

The targets selected for the **DAY** and **NIGHT** sections determine where a call that hits this Day Night Mode target will route next, depending on the mode the target is in.

When you have finished setting up the target, click on the **Save** button followed by the orange-colored **Apply Configuration Changes** bar.

Once the target has been saved, it will be visible in the menu bar on the right side of the page. Targets listed in red are in the Night mode. Targets in green are in the Day mode:

Add Day/Night Code
(*280)
(*281)
(*282)

In this example, the **Day Night Mode** targets with the indexes zero and one are in Night mode and the target with index two is in Day mode.

Phonebook Directory

Phonebook Directory targets do not require setting up any additional configuration beyond initial user setup. The Phonebook Directory allows a caller to search for a user's extension by dialing the first three letters of their first, last, or first and last name. As long as the user has the Voicemail & Directory option enabled, they will be listed in the directory.

The **Phonebook Directory** has a few options that are configurable on the **General Settings** page. To configure these options, click on the General Settings link under the **Basic** header in the FreePBX navigation menu:

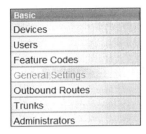

Scroll down to the **Company Directory** section to locate all directory options:

The **Find users in the Company Directory by** option allows the directory to be searched by first name, last name, or both.

When **Announce Extension** is enabled, it will play a message stating the extension number of the person who is being called after the caller has located them in the directory.

The value of **Operator Extension** is the extension or target that the caller will be routed to if they press *0* while in the directory. This could be a direct extension, an external telephone number, or the number for a ring group or queue. If nothing is entered into this field, FreePBX will attempt to route the caller back to the target they came from before entering the directory. If there was no previous target, the caller is played a message stating that they have pressed an invalid option.

If you changed any options on this page, be sure to click on the **Submit Changes** button at the bottom of the page, followed by the orange-colored **Apply Configuration Changes** bar.

Summary

By this point, we should have a good understanding of each of the different types of basic call targets, and should likely have several targets set up and ready to accept calls. We should be able to create call targets in order to do the following:

- Terminate calls
- Ring an extension directly
- Drop a call directly to voicemail (without ringing an extension first)
- Ring a group of phones using various ring strategies
- Conference multiple users together
- Route calls between two different destinations using Day Night Mode controls
- Search the phonebook directory for all users with a voicemail box on the system

In the next chapter, we will cover the advanced call targets of queues, time conditions, and IVRs.

6
Advanced Call Targets

Advanced call targets in FreePBX require a bit of additional set up before they can be used. They often generate complicated call flows. However, for the most part, FreePBX developers have encapsulated this complexity into a straightforward interface. Advanced call targets allow callers to be directed to queues (so that a caller hears music until all of the calls in front of them have been cleared and someone is available to take their call), or to digital receptionists routing calls based on input from the caller. Advanced call targets also allow calls to take different paths depending on the date, day of the week, or time of the day.

In this chapter, we will be discussing advanced call targets in FreePBX, which are as follows:

- Queues
- Time Conditions
- IVR (Digital Receptionist)

Queue

A queue is a "line up" or "stack" of calls that need to be answered. By default, FreePBX queues work in a First In, First Out (FIFO) fashion (the first caller who enters the queue is the first caller to be picked up out of the queue). Call queues are useful for scenarios in which the volume of callers is expected to exceed the number of people available to answer calls. Scenarios such as a technical support line or a sales line are good examples. Callers who are placed into a queue will hear music while on hold until someone is available to answer their call. It is often helpful to think of queues in terms of a physical store, wherein, there are a small number of employees to serve a large number of people. Imagine you are in a line at the bank with ten other people and there are only three tellers. The three tellers are unable to serve all of the ten people at once, and it would be rude for them to help someone from the middle of the line before the person who is next in the line.

Each person is called up to an available teller in the order that they entered the line. In North America, this is generally called "waiting in line", but in some countries this is actually referred to as a queue. Such is the case with a telephone queue. If you are the fifth caller to enter a queue, then you will be the fifth caller to be picked up by an available user.

Queue Priorities

By default, any queue created in FreePBX will treat callers with a FIFO methodology. However, there may be situations, when certain callers should be prioritized in order to enable shorter wait times. Going back to the analogy of a physical bank, those ten customers waiting in line may see a new customer enter the bank and walk straight past the line to be serviced by an available teller. The customer may be a business customer instead of a personal banking customer, or they may simply be paying for a higher level of service. Whatever the case may be, they are allowed to bypass all of the other customers in order to receive faster service. Queue priorities allow particular callers to be weighted differently than others, in order to enable this kind of prioritization.

The default setting for all of the callers is to have a priority of zero. Callers with a priority above zero will be placed in front of priority zero callers. The highest priority call will be placed first when ordering calls in the queue, and the order will be decided by descending priority. Queue priorities are often used when **service level agreements (SLAs)** are present, which stipulate that certain callers must have their call answered within a certain timeframe. Setting those callers up with a higher priority will ensure they are placed at the front of the queue and that their call will be answered more quickly than calls from those without SLAs. FreePBX allows call priorities to be set between zero and twenty.

Queue priorities act as their own call target. A caller is directed to a queue priority target and is then immediately redirected to another call target. Once passing through a queue priority target, a call will hold its newly assigned priority for any queue that it enters (a caller only needs to be prioritized once, after which they can enter as many queues as they need to without fear of losing their priority number).

In order to set up a new queue priority target, click on the **Queue Priorities** link in the navigation menu on the left as shown in the following screenshot:

The queue priorities edit screen will be displayed as follows:

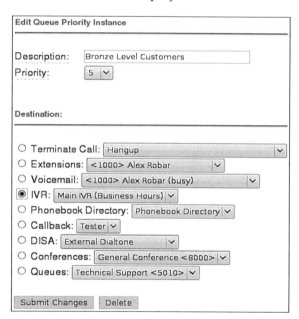

The edit screen has two main sections as follows:

- **Edit Queue Priority Instance**
- **Destination**

The first section allows for a description (used when selecting this priority as a target) and the actual priority itself. In this example, the queue priority is being set up in order to prioritize bronze level callers. Callers are given a priority of **5**, placing them above callers with no priority, but leaving plenty of room for callers with a higher-level SLA.

The **Destination** section is for selecting the call target that the caller will be sent to, now that they are prioritized. Queue priorities that do not have queues as their eventual destinations are essentially useless. So, be sure that the caller will eventually wind up in a queue if they are sent through a queue priority target. This usually means sending the caller directly to a queue or an IVR where a queue is a possible option.

When the **Description**, **Priority**, and **Destination** fields have been set, click on the **Submit Changes** button in order to save the priority, and then click on the orange-colored **Apply Configuration Changes** bar in order to have the changes take effect.

Queue priorities are usually set up as the first call target for inbound calls. Inbound routes can be set up in order to recognize a particular caller's caller ID and then route them to the appropriate call priority. Alternatively, if customers are given different phone numbers to call based upon their service level, then an inbound route can send calls to those numbers to specific queue priorities.

Queues

Queues can be very simple to set up for basic functionality, but advanced options and behaviors come with a bit of a learning curve. Queues have over thirty options, making them the most complicated call target available in FreePBX.

In order to set up a new queue, click on the **Queues** link in the navigation menu on the left as shown in the following screenshot:

The **Add Queue** screen will be displayed with a section that has five options: **Add Queue, Queue Options, Caller Position Announcements, Periodic Announcements**, and **Fail Over Destination**.

Add Queue

The **Add Queue** section has seven options and an **Extension Quick Pick** drop-down menu as shown in the following screenshot:

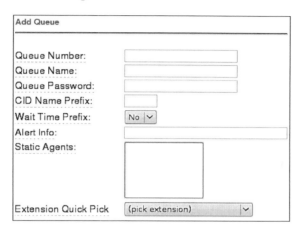

Queue Number can be thought of as the "extension" assigned to the queue. If a caller is calling into the queue from an endpoint on this system, or someone is transferring a call to the queue, then this is the number they will use. The **Queue Number** is also used to sign in and out of the queue. If an employee is not permanently a member of the queue, they can dial this **Queue Number** plus * to log into the queue, and this **Queue Number** plus ** to log out (for example, a Queue Number of 5000 would have agents dial 5000* to log in and 5000** to log out).

Queue Name is used to identify the queue when selecting it as a call target. This name is not parsed by FreePBX.

If **Queue Password** is not left blank then queue agents will be required to enter this password before they are able to join the queue. This option is used in conjunction with the **Queue Number** (agents will be prompted for the password after dialing the **Queue Number** plus *). This setting is optional.

The **CID Name Prefix** is used to prefix the caller ID of callers in the queue with the value entered in this field. This is often used when agents are members of multiple queues so that they know which department a person has called (for example, a CID may be prefixed with "Sales" or "Tech Support").

Wait Time Prefix is used to prefix the caller ID of callers in the queue with the number of minutes the caller has been waiting in the queue. The time will be rounded off to the nearest minute, and will be prefixed with the letter "M". If the call is subsequently transferred to another queue with this feature set, the time count will reset.

Alert Info is used to send specific ALERT_INFO SIP headers to SIP endpoints that support them. Many SIP endpoints can be set up to ring differently, or automatically answer calls when specific ALERT_INFO values are received. For ALERT_INFO headers to trigger an action on an endpoint, the ALERT_INFO header that the phone is configured to look for must match the ALERT_INFO header that FreePBX is sending. Some endpoints will allow the information headers to be configured on the device, while others have these header values statically configured so they cannot be changed. The documentation that accompanies a SIP endpoint should list whether or not the device supports ALERT_INFO headers, as well as if the headers can be configured, or are predefined.

Static Agents are extensions that are always members of the queue. Static agents do not need to log into the queue, and cannot log out of the queue. As long as an agent listed in this field is available, their endpoint will be rung when a caller is in this queue. Extensions should be listed one per line. Remote telephone numbers or extensions can also be added to this field. Note that unlike ring groups, external numbers can be added as they would be dialed from a normal endpoint on the system, and do not require a pound symbol at the end.

Advanced users can add agents from their /etc/asterisk/agents.conf file to the **Static Agents** field by prefixing their agent number with the letter "A" (for example, agent number 2223 would be listed as A2223). For the time being, this functionality is considered experimental and may cause various issues with terminating and transferring calls that are received by these agents.

Any agent listed in the Static Agents field can have a penalty value appended to their extension after a comma (for example, agent 2223 with a penalty value of 1 would be listed as "2223,1"). Listing an agent without a penalty value assigns the agent a penalty of zero. Penalties affect when certain agents are called. The higher the penalty an agent has, the less likely they are to receive a call from the queue. An agent with a penalty of one will only be rung if nobody with a penalty of zero is available. Likewise, an agent with a penalty of two will only be rung if nobody with a penalty of zero or one is available. Penalties are useful for adding agents to the queue who would not normally be taking these type of calls, but should be available to handle overflow of calls if the need arises.

The **Extension Quick Pick** list allows any configured extension to be selected from the drop-down menu. The selected extension will be copied into the **Static Agents** field with a penalty of zero.

Queue Options

The **Queue Options** section has just under twenty options available for configuring the queue as shown in the following screenshot:

The **Agent Announcement** drop-down menu is used to select a sound file to be played back to the agent who answers the call before the call is bridged to them. This file must be pre-recorded or uploaded to the system through the **System Recordings** FreePBX section (more information on creating custom recordings for the Agent Announcement field can be found in the *Custom Voice Prompts* section in Chapter 9, *Personalizing Your PBX*). This announcement is optional, but may serve the purpose of telling the agent which queue the call came from (if CID is not available to provide this information).

The **Join Announcement** drop-down menu is used to select a sound file to be played back to the caller before they are dropped into the queue. This file must be pre-recorded or uploaded to the system through the **System Recordings** section of FreePBX. This announcement is optional, but will usually state that the caller is being placed into a queue, and that their call will be answered in priority sequence.

The **Music on Hold Class** drop-down menu is used to configure the music that is played to the caller while they wait in the queue. The **inherit** option can be selected in order to have the queue use the same music on hold class already assigned to the call (usually this is set through an inbound route). Music on hold classes can be configured in the **Music on Hold** section of FreePBX (more information on creating custom recordings for the **Agent Announcement** field can be found in the *Custom Music on Hold* section in Chapter 9).

If the **Ringing Instead of MoH** box is checked then callers will hear ringing instead of Music on Hold while they wait in a queue. Use this option carefully; a long wait time can mean dozens of ring tones and often a caller who hangs up (thinking their call is never going to be answered). If this option is enabled, the option selected in the **Music on Hold Class** drop-down menu is ignored.

Max Wait Time is the amount of time that a caller is able to wait in the queue before the call is considered failed and routed to the failover destination. Set it to **Unlimited** in order to configure the queue to use an unlimited wait time. This field has a maximum value of one hour otherwise.

Max Callers is the maximum number of callers allowed to enter the queue at any time. Callers over this limit will immediately be sent to the failover destination. Enter **0** to configure the queue for an unlimited number of callers. This field has a maximum value of 50 otherwise.

If **Join Empty** is set to **Yes**, then callers are able to join the queue and wait even if no agents are signed into the queue. The **Strict** option will not allow callers to join the queue if either no agents are signed in or all of the signed in agents are unavailable. The **No** option will not let callers join the queue if no agents are signed in, but it *will* allow callers to join if all of the signed in agents are unavailable. Callers that are not allowed to join the queue because of Strict or No settings are immediately sent to the failover destination.

The **Leave When Empty** drop-down menu carries the same settings as the **Join Empty** drop-down menu. Leave When Empty is employed when there are suddenly no more agents signed into the queue *after* a caller has already joined the queue.

The **Ring Strategy** drop-down menu determines the way that agents will be called when a caller enters the queue. It has the following options:

- **ringall**: All of the agents are rung until one answers.

- **roundrobin**: Agents are rung one at a time in the order they are listed in the **Ring Strategy** textbox until one of them picks up.

- **leastrecent**: It is similar to **roundrobin**, but starts with the agent who was least recently called by this queue. Note that FreePBX does not account for call length, so the timer that counts how long ago an agent was rung starts counting from when an agent picks up a call, not from when the call is completed. An agent who is on a call for an hour is still considered to have been rung an hour ago.

- **fewestcalls**: Rings the agent who has answered the fewest calls from this queue.

- **random**: Rings a random agent.

- **rrmemory**: It is similar to **roundrobin**, but remembers the last agent who was rung in the last round robin and starts by calling them first.

Agent Timeout is the number of seconds an agent's phone can ring before the call is considered failed for that agent. Set this to **Unlimited** in order to ring the agents continuously until somebody answers the call. This field has a maximum value of 60 seconds otherwise. Note that this field will be overridden if either the general ring time setting or an extension's own follow-me ring time setting is lower than the specified timeout. For example, if the FreePBX general ring time setting is set to 30 seconds, and **Agent Timeout** is set to 45 seconds, then the maximum amount of time that an agents phone will ring is 30 seconds. Also, setting this field to **Unlimited** will only work for the **ringall** ring strategy. Other strategies will ring extensions for 60 seconds (or the value of the general ring time setting or the extension's follow-me ring time, whichever is shorter) before carrying on to ring the next agent.

The **Retry** value is the number of seconds the system will wait before calling an agent after the last attempt timed out. Selecting **No Retry** will send the caller to the failover destination as soon as the first attempted agent times out (additional agents will not be rung). This field has a maximum value of 20 seconds.

Wrap-Up-Time is the number of seconds an agent is considered unavailable after they have completed a call from this queue. Setting this option to **0 seconds** means no delay. This field has a maximum value of 60 seconds.

If **Call Recording** is not set to **No** then calls to this queue will be recorded in the selected format and saved to `/var/spool/asterisk/monitor`. Calls to a queue that are recorded will be named using the format: `q(QueueNumber)-(Date)-(Time)-(CallID).(Format)`. The tokens should be replaced with the following values to locate the file:

Token	Replaced with
(QueueNumber)	The number or extension of the queue. The number of the queue is configured in the **Queue Number** field.
(Date)	The date that the call was answered on. The date is in the format of YYYYMMDD.
(Time)	The time that the call was answered. The time is in the format of HHMMSS, and is in 24 hour format.
(CallID)	A unique ID assigned to the call by FreePBX. The ID is not referenced anywhere in the FreePBX interface. Hence, if two calls come into the same queue at the exact same time, they will have to be heard in order to determine which call is which.
(Format)	The appropriate file extension for the format of the call. WAV and WAV49 formats will have an extension of `.wav`; the GSM format has an extension of `.gsm`.

For example, a call that came into queue number 11 on July 19, 2009 at 7:05:45 p.m. might have a filename of `q11-20090715-190545-1247699145.4355.wav`.

If **Event When Called** is set to **Yes**, the events generated in the **Asterisk Manager Interface (AMI)** during the progress of a call to this queue include AgentCalled, AgentDump, AgentConnect, and AgentComplete. AMI events can be used by third-party software programs in order to track call progress and generate call metrics.

Similar to **Event When Called**, when **Member Status** is set to **Yes** the QueueMemberStatus event will be generated in the AMI during call progress.

If **Skip Busy Agents** is set to **Yes**, then agents who are on a call will not be rung when there is a caller in the queue. This option applies to extensions with call waiting active, or multi-line endpoints. Even though these endpoints have the ability to receive multiple calls at the same time, if they are in use they will not be rung.

Queue Weight gives all of the callers in the queue a particular priority. This weighting is used by Asterisk to determine which call to deliver to agents signed into multiple queues. If an agent is signed into multiple queues and both queues have callers waiting in them, the queue with the higher Queue Weight will ring through to the agent first.

The **Autofill** option is only applicable to Asterisk version 1.4 and later versions. This option allows multiple callers to be sent to multiple agents at the same time. For example, if three callers are in the queue, and three agents are available, enabling this option will send each caller to one of the agents. If this option is disabled then only one call is processed at a time, and every caller must wait to be first in line before any agent is rung for their call. This option has no effect in Asterisk version 1.2. This option is not affected by the selected ring strategy (agents are still rung in the order defined by the ring strategy).

The **Agent Regex Filter** can be used to restrict the extensions of agents who are allowed to sign into the queue. If this field is left blank then it is possible for any agent who knows the queue number and password to sign into the queue. Entering a regular expression in this field can restrict the agents who can log into the queue to specific extensions or ranges of extensions.

Regular expressions can be very complicated. It is a good idea to have a thorough understanding of how to craft regular expressions before attempting to use the **Agent Regex Filter** field. An invalid regular expression in this field could make the queue entirely inaccessible to all of the agents. More information on regular expressions can be found at http://en.wikipedia.org/wiki/Regular_expression.

Caller Position Announcements

The **Caller Position Announcements** section has three configurable options as shown in the following screenshot:

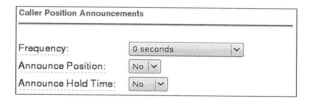

This section is used to control how often a message is played to each caller in the queue detailing their position in the queue and how long it is estimated that they will be on hold.

The **Frequency** drop-down menu controls how often this type of announcement is made. Setting this to **0 seconds** disables the announcements entirely. This field has a maximum value of 20 minutes otherwise.

If **Announce Position** is set to **Yes** then the caller will be told their place in the queue each time the position announcement is played.

If **Announce Hold Time** is set to **Yes**, then the caller will be told their estimated hold time each time this message is played. If this field is set to **Only Once**, then the estimated hold time will be played to the caller when they first join the queue, but never again. When estimated hold times are less than one minute, hold times are not announced.

If both **Announce Position** and **Announce Hold Time** are set to **No**, neither announcement will ever be played no matter what the **Frequency** field is set to.

Periodic Announcements

Periodic announcements can be played to each caller in order to give them the option to perform another task. Usually this means that an IVR is presented to the caller, and the caller is given the option to leave a voicemail or to reach a different department. The **Periodic Announcements** section has two configurable options as shown in the following screenshot:

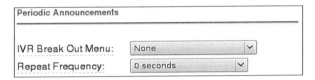

IVR Break Out Menu is the IVR that should be presented to the caller each time the announcement is played. The recording set for the selected IVR is what will be played to the caller. The selected IVR must only contain single-digit options.

Repeat Frequency is how often the IVR should be presented to the caller. Setting this to **0 seconds** disables the periodic announcements. This field has a maximum value of 20 minutes otherwise.

The user can only select one **Fail Over Destination** as shown in the following screenshot:

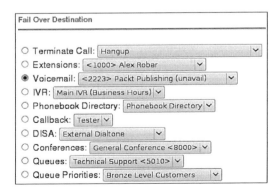

Select the call target where callers should be directed if their call to this queue fails for any reason. A call could be considered failed because no agents were signed into the queue, the caller waited in the queue for too long, or no signed in agents were available to answer the call (depending on the configured options).

 The previous screenshot references a few targets that we have not yet discussed. The **Callback** and **DISA** targets are not discussed in this chapter. More information on both targets can be found in Chapter 9.

When all of the options have been configured for the desired queue behavior, click on the **Submit Changes** button in order to save the queue, and then click on the orange-colored **Apply Configuration Changes** bar in order to load the queue into the running Asterisk configuration.

Time conditions

Time conditions are a set of rules for hours, dates, or days of the week. A condition has two call targets each time. Calls sent to a time condition will be sent to one target if the time of the call matches one of the conditions, or to the other target if none of the conditions match. Each time condition can have multiple time definitions (known as time groups). Time conditions are often used to control how a phone system responds to callers inside and outside of business hours, and during holidays.

Time Groups

Before we can set up a time condition call target, we need to define a set of time groups. Time groups are a list of rules against which incoming calls are checked. The rules specify a specific date or time, and a call can be routed differently if the time it comes in matches with one of the rules in a time group. Each time group can have an unlimited number of rules defined. It is useful to group similar sets of time rules together. For example, there may be one time group for business hours in which the time that the business will be open will be defined. Another popular time group is for holidays, in which each holiday that falls on a business day is defined.

In order to create a new time group, click on the **Time Groups** link in the navigation menu on the left as shown in the following screenshot:

The **Add Time Group** screen will be displayed as shown in the following screenshot:

The **Description** field is used to identify this time group, when selecting it during the setup of a time condition. This value is not parsed by FreePBX.

The **New Time** section is used to define a time rule that a call will be matched against. Leaving a field as the default dash (-) will match all of the values (for example, **Week Day Start** to **Week Day Finish** will match on every day of the week). Keep in mind that all of the conditions must be true for the rule to match, so it is possible to create rules that never match (setting **Month Day start** and **Month Day finish** to 31 and **Month start** and **Month finish** to September will never match as there is no 31st of September).

Once the appropriate rule has been defined, click on the **Submit** button in order to save the rule. Additional time rules can be added to a time group by clicking on the group's name in the time group list on the right and selecting additional rule parameters in the **New Time** section at the bottom of the page. An example of a time group with multiple rules might be a group defining business hours as shown in the following screenshot:

Time Group

Description   Business Hours

08:30-17:30|mon-fri|*|*

Time to start: 08 : 30
Time to finish: 17 : 30
Week Day Start: Monday
Week Day finish: Friday
Month Day start: -
Month Day finish: -
Month start: -
Month finish: -

10:00-16:30|sat|*|*

Time to start: 10 : 00
Time to finish: 16 : 30
Week Day Start: Saturday
Week Day finish: Saturday
Month Day start: -
Month Day finish: -
Month start: -
Month finish: -

In this example, the condition will match Monday through Friday, 8:30 a.m. through 5:30 p.m. and on Saturday from 10:00 a.m. through 4:30 p.m.

Time Conditions

Once a time group has been defined, a time condition can be set up as a call target. In order to create a new time condition, click on the **Time Conditions** link in the navigation menu on the left as shown in the following screenshot:

The **Add Time Condition** screen will be displayed along with four configuration sections. The first section is the **Add Time Condition** section as shown in the following screenshot:

The **Time Condition name** field is used for identifying the time condition when selecting it as a call target. This value is not parsed by FreePBX.

The **Time Group** drop-down menu is used to select the time group that this time condition should be referencing for time rules. When a call reaches this time condition, the rules in the selected Time Group will be parsed in order to determine where to send the call next.

The **Day/Night Mode Association** section has only one configurable option as shown in the following screenshot. Click on the **Submit Changes** button in order to save the queue, and then click on the orange-colored **Apply Configuration Changes** bar to load the queue into the running Asterisk configuration.

If desired, a day/night mode call target can be directly associated with this time condition through the **Associate with** drop-down menu. Associating a day/night mode target with a time condition allows the time condition to be overridden by triggering the day/night mode. When selecting the day/night mode association, each day/night mode that has been configured will be available twice in the **Associate with** drop-down menu — once as **Force Night** and the second time as **Force Day**.

The option selected in this drop-down menu will configure which mode the day/night mode target must be in for the time condition to be overridden. In the previous example, the **Bad Weather** day/night mode has been selected with the **Force Night** option. If inclement weather forces someone to toggle Bad Weather into night mode, then any calls landing on this time condition will be sent to the night destination associated with Bad Weather, no matter what date or time the call is coming in. As soon as Bad Weather is toggled back to day mode, calls will be processed through this time condition according to the rules set up in the selected time group.

The last two sections, **Destination if time matches** and **Destination if time does not match** (as shown in the following screenshot) are for setting up the call targets for calls that match the rules set up in the selected time group and for calls that do not:

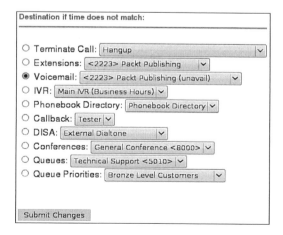

Select the desired call destinations, click on the **Submit Changes** button in order to save the destination, and then click on the orange-colored **Apply Configuration Changes** bar in order to load the destination into the running Asterisk configuration.

IVR (Digital Receptionist)

An **Interactive Voice Response (IVR)** system is often referred to as a digital receptionist. An IVR plays back a pre-recorded message to the caller that asks them to press various buttons on their telephone depending on which department or person they would like to speak with. The IVR system will then route the call accordingly.

FreePBX IVRs allow any digits to be defined as destinations (for example, pressing one might route to the sales ring group). A destination of **t** can also be defined to route the call if the IVR times out without receiving any input. A destination of **i** can be defined to route the call if the IVR receives invalid input.

In order to create an IVR, click on the **IVR** link in the navigation menu on the left as shown in the following screenshot:

The **Digital Receptionist** screen will appear with two configuration sections: **IVR options** and **IVR destinations**. The **IVR options** section has a dozen configurable options as shown in the following screenshot:

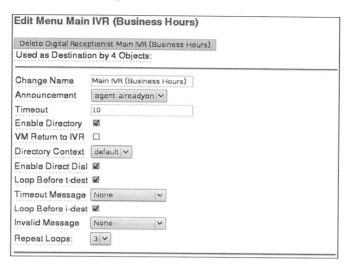

Change Name is used as a name for identifying the IVR. This field is not parsed by FreePBX.

The **Announcement** drop-down menu is used to select a pre-recorded message that will be played to the caller as they enter the IVR. Recordings must be pre-recorded or updated in the **System Recordings** FreePBX section.

Timeout is the number of seconds that the system will wait for input from the caller. If this number of seconds passes without input, the call will fail over to the **t** destination (if defined), or the call will be disconnected.

If **Enable Directory** is checked then callers can press the pound (#) key to enter a directory system that will allow them to search for a person by first name or last name. Otherwise, pressing the pound key will play back a message stating that the caller has provided invalid input.

If **VM Return to IVR** is checked then a caller who transfers from the IVR to a voicemail box will be transferred back to the IVR when they are done leaving a message. If this option is not selected then the caller will be disconnected after leaving a voicemail.

If multiple directory contexts are defined, the directory that should be accessible to the caller when the pound key is pressed can be selected from the **Directory Context** drop-down menu.

The **Enable Direct Dial** option enables the callers to dial an extension directly from the IVR. If this option is disabled then the callers will receive a message stating that they have provided invalid input when they enter an extension, *even if the extension is valid*.

If the **Loop Before t-dest** box is checked then the IVR will loop back to the start of itself after a timeout is reached. The IVR will loop for as many times as is selected in the **Repeat Loops** drop-down menu. If this option is not selected, then a caller who times out once will be immediately transferred to the **t** destination if it is defined or will be disconnected otherwise.

Timeout Message is the message that will be played to the caller if they fail to enter any input before the number of seconds specified in the **Timeout** box. This message will only be played if the **t** destination is not defined.

Loop Before i-dest works in the same way as the **Loop Before t-dest** checkbox, except this option checks for invalid input. If invalid input is entered when this box is checked, the IVR will loop. Otherwise, the IVR will fail over to the **i** destination, or disconnect if the **i** destination does not exist.

Invalid Message is the message that will be played to the caller if they enter invalid options while in the IVR. This message will only be played if the **i** destination is not defined.

Repeat Loops is used to select the number of times the IVR will repeat itself when no valid input is received. After the specified number of loops, the caller will be disconnected. The maximum number of loops allowed is nine.

The **IVR destinations** section (as shown in the following screenshot) allows key presses to be mapped to specific destinations:

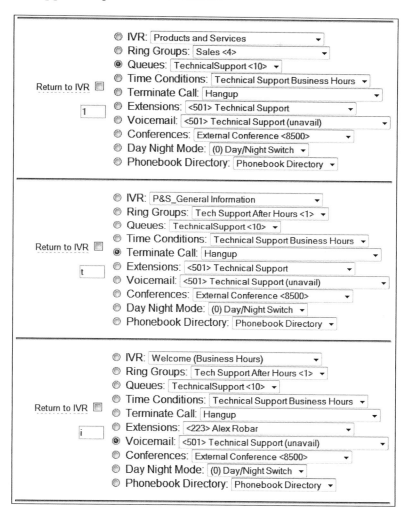

In this example, pressing 1 will route the caller to the **Technical Support** queue, timing out (the **t** destination) will disconnect the caller, and entering invalid input (the **i** destination) will drop the caller to voicemail box number 501. Additional options can be added by clicking on the **Increase Options** button. An IVR can have as many options as required, including multi-digit destinations. Keep in mind that when using multi-digit destinations, the system will wait until a timeout has reached when a single digit is pressed (for example, a system that allows the caller to press 1, 10, 11, and 12 will force the caller to wait for a timeout when just 1 is pressed).

When all of the IVR options are configured for the desired behavior, click on the **Save** button to save the IVR, and then click on the orange-colored **Apply Configuration Changes** bar to load the IVR into the running Asterisk configuration.

Summary

By this point, we should have a good understanding of advanced call targets. We should be able to route calls using complicated time conditions into an IVR system that eventually routes the caller into a call queue, if we desire to do so.

The next chapter will put our call targets into action with inbound call routes. We will also discuss setting up outbound routes (in order to utilize the trunks we set up a few chapters ago), in addition to setting up least cost routing in order to properly route calls over the cheapest available trunk.

7
Call Routing

Up until this point, we have discussed various call targets and what will happen to calls when they reach those targets.

In this chapter, we will discuss the following:

- Inbound routing
- Follow Me and the VmX Locater
- Outbound routing
- Least Cost Routing (the ability to pick the cheapest route for a call, based on the dialed destination)

Inbound routing

Inbound routing is one of the key pieces to a functional Asterisk phone system. Inbound routes in FreePBX are where we finally get to put the call targets discussed in Chapters 5 and 6 to use. FreePBX allows two specific types of inbound routing:

- DID-based routing: DID-based routing routes calls based on the trunk on which the call is coming in. CID-based routing routes calls based on the caller ID number of the person who is calling. Within those two routing methods, FreePBX allows the detection of inbound faxes. **DID (Direct Inward Dialing)**, in VoIP telephony, refers to a trunk and the telephone number associated with that trunk. As it is possible for a phone system to have several trunks, FreePBX allows different routing rules to be set up for each trunk. This is commonly used when a company has a dedicated technical support phone number (which routes directly to their support department), while other calls to the company come in to a different phone number and are routed to an IVR or a receptionist.

- CID-based routing: **CID (caller ID)** refers to the name and number of the person calling. FreePBX allows inbound calls to be routed based on the number someone is calling from. This is commonly used to immediately disconnect calls from known telemarketers, but can also be used to route calls from specific people in a different way than routing calls from the general public.

These two routing methods can be used on their own or in conjunction with one another.

To set up inbound routing, click on the **Inbound Routes** link in the navigation menu under the **Inbound Call Control** section:

Six sections are present on the **Add Incoming Route** page:

1. **Add Incoming Route**
2. **Options**
3. **Privacy**
4. **Fax Handling**
5. **CID Lookup Source**
6. **Set Destination**

The **Add Incoming Route** section has the following four options:

1. **Description**
2. **DID Number**
3. **Caller ID Number**
4. **CID Priority Route**

```
Add Incoming Route

Description:          [                    ]
DID Number:          [                    ]
Caller ID Number:    [                    ]
CID Priority Route:   □
```

The **Description** field is used to hold a description to help you remember what this particular inbound route is for. This field is not parsed by FreePBX.

The **DID Number** field is used when DID-based routing is desired. The phone number of the DID to be matched should be entered in this field. The DID number *must* match the format in which the provider is sending the DID. Many providers will send the DID information with the call as +15555555555, while others will leave out the country code information and simply send 5555555555. If the DID entered in this field does not exactly match with the number sent by the provider, then the inbound route will not be used.

This field can be left blank to match calls from all DIDs (this will also match calls that have no DID information).

This field also allows patterns to match a range of numbers. Patterns must begin with an underscore (_) to signify that they are patterns. Within patterns, x will match the numbers 0 through 9, and specific numbers can be matched if they are placed between square parentheses. For example, to match both 555-555-1234 and 555-555-1235, the pattern would be _555555123[45].

The **Caller ID Number** field is used when CID-based routing is desired. As with the DID Number field, the CID entered in this field must exactly match the format in which the provider is sending the CID. Providers may send 7, 10, or 11 digits; they may include a country code and the plus symbol. Check with your provider to see the format in which the CID is sent, in order to ensure that the field is entered correctly.

The Caller ID Number field can be left blank to match with all CIDs (this will also match calls that have no CID information sent with them). The field allows **Private**, **Blocked**, **Unknown**, **Restricted**, **Anonymous**, and **Unavailable** values to be entered, as many providers will send these in the CID number data.

Leaving both the DID Number and Caller ID Number fields blank will create a route that matches all calls.

Inbound routing priorities

It is possible to run into a situation in which a call matches several of the defined inbound routes. In this scenario, FreePBX will give a route priority in the following sequence:

1. Routes with a specific DID and CID will always be first in priority.
2. Routes with a specific DID but no CID will be second in priority.
3. Routes with no DID, but with a specific CID will be third in priority.
4. Routes with no specific DID or CID will be last in priority.

It is important to note that by default, setting up a route for a specific DID will take preference over setting up a route for a specific CID.

The **CID Priority Route** toggle affects the inbound routing priority behavior. If this checkbox is selected, all calls from the number specified in the **Caller ID Number** field will be routed using the route even if there is a route for the DID on which the call came in. If there is a specific route that specifies both DID and CID, then that route will still take precedence. Checking the CID Priority Route toggle simply swaps the second and third routing priorities for this particular route.

The **Options** section has five fields as shown in the following screenshot:

Alert Info is used to send a string of text in the SIP ALERT_INFO headers. This is often used for SIP endpoints that ring differently, or auto-answer calls based on the ALERT_INFO text that is received. Any inbound call that matches this route will send the text in this field to any SIP device that receives the call.

The **CID name prefix** field allows text to be prepended to the caller ID name information from the call. This is often used to identify where a call came from (calls to a number dedicated for technical support might be prefixed with "Tech").

The **Music On Hold** drop-down menu allows the music-on-hold class for this call to be selected. Whenever a caller who passes through this route is placed on hold, they will hear the music on hold defined in the class selected here. This is often used for companies that advertise in their music on hold and accept calls in multiple different languages. Calls to a French DID might play a music-on-hold class with French advertisements, while an English DID would play a class with English advertisements.

The **Signal RINGING** toggle will send "ringing" in the call progress data, before Asterisk lets the other side know that the call has been answered. Some providers require this, while this can break functionality with others. Check with your provider to see if they require "ringing" to be sent as a call progress before the call is answered.

The **Pause Before Answer** field contains the number of seconds that Asterisk should pause before answering the call. This is not useful for digital channels, but analog ZAP channels may have security systems or fax machines installed in parallel with the VoIP system. In such cases, a tone is usually played within a few seconds of the call being picked up to identify that the call is not a voice call. Setting a delay of a few seconds allows this tone to be played and the other piece of equipment to seize the line for communications. If the line has not been picked up by the end of this delay, Asterisk will answer the call.

The **Privacy** section only has one configurable field:

Privacy	
Privacy Manager:	No

The **Privacy Manager** drop-down menu is used to enable or disable the FreePBX privacy manager functionality. When enabled, calls that come in without an associated caller ID number will be prompted to enter their 10-digit telephone number. Callers will be given three attempts to enter this information before their call is disconnected.

The **Fax Handling** section has four configurable fields:

Fax Handling	
Fax Extension:	FreePBX default
Fax Email:	
Fax Detection Type:	None
Pause After Answer:	

The **Fax Extension** dropdown is used to select the extension that the inbound faxes will be directed to. Typically, this extension is a ZAP/DAHDI extension that has a physical fax machine plugged into it. However, it may also be a virtual extension answered by a software program on the PBX. The program will accept faxes and turn them into digital documents for review.

If **disabled** is selected, fax detection will not be used for calls that match this route. Any fax calls will be routed just like voice calls.

If **FreePBX default** is selected, faxes will be routed to the extension defined on the FreePBX **General Settings** page.

If **system** is selected, faxes will be received by FreePBX and emailed to the address specified in the **Fax Email** field shown in the previous screenshot. If the Fax Email field is left blank, the fax email address specified on the FreePBX General Settings page will be used.

The **Fax Detection Type** drop-down menu determines which type of detection mechanism Asterisk will use to detect the fax:

- **None**: This option disables fax detection
- **Zaptel**: This option should be used when the fax is coming from a ZAP trunk
- **NVFax**: This option should be used when the fax is coming from a SIP or IAX2 trunk

Selecting Zaptel or NVFax will cause Asterisk to immediately answer the call and then listen for fax tones. Asterisk will listen for fax tones for the number of seconds defined in the **Pause After Answer** field. If no tones are heard within this time frame, the call is considered to be a voice call.

The **CID Lookup Source** section only has one configurable field as shown in the following screenshot:

The **Source** drop-down menu allows any predefined lookup source to be selected. Any calls that match this route will be checked against the source specified here, and will have their caller ID name changed if they match an entry in the source. Caller ID lookup sources are specified on the FreePBX **CallerID Lookup Sources** page (more information on CallerID Lookup Sources can be found in the *CallerID Lookup Sources* section of Chapter 9, *Personalizing Your PBX*).

Lastly, the **Set Destination** section has one option to configure:

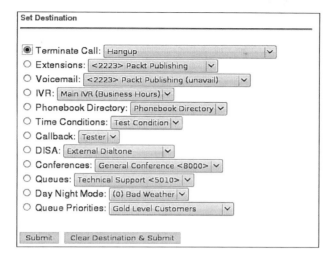

This is the place where the desired call target is selected. Any previously set up call target can be selected including extensions, IVRs, time conditions, conference rooms, and queues.

When all options have been selected, click on the **Submit** button to save the route. Clicking on the **Clear Destination & Submit** button will save the route without any associated destination. This is generally used for fax-only routes, where a fax must be detected or the call will be terminated. Once the route has been saved, be sure to click on the orange-colored **Apply Configuration Changes** bar at the top of the screen to make the route active.

Follow Me and the VmX Locater

Follow Me will force Asterisk to try and track a user down when their extension is called instead of simply ringing their assigned endpoint. This is often used to call a cell phone before dropping the caller to voicemail. With this enabled, the user never needs to give out their cell number because the system will always try to reach them there when their main endpoint is not answered. Likewise, if the cell number changes it simply has to be updated in one place and no calls are missed.

FreePBX has two implementations of the "follow-me" system—the default Follow Me and the VmX Locater.

The default follow-me system is controlled by the FreePBX administrator, and allows for varying ring strategies, ring times, music-on-hold selections, and various other complex settings. The VmX Locater is controlled by the end user, but is a much simpler implementation that consists of prompting the caller to press 0, 1, or 2 and directing calls to different numbers based on what was selected.

Default Follow Me

The default follow-me routing will ring a set number of extensions in a pre-selected ring pattern (similar to a ring group) before failing over to another call target. This could mean that several VoIP phones and a cell phone are rung at the same time, or they might be rung in order, until one of them picks up. If there is no answer, the call could fail over to voicemail, or be redirected to another person at the company.

To set up default follow-me routing in FreePBX, click on the **Follow Me** link in the navigation menu under the **Inbound Call Control** section:

Click on the user that requires Follow Me settings in the list on the right and the
Follow Me screen is displayed as shown in the following screenshot:

The **Disable** checkbox will temporarily disable the follow-me setup while retaining
the follow-me configuration. Any calls that are direct dial calls or calls that come
from an IVR or a directory search will ring the extension directly instead of using the
follow-me routing. Note that if follow me is specifically selected as a call target, the
follow-me route will be respected for that call, regardless of whether this checkbox
is selected.

The **Initial Ring Time** field is used to configure the number of seconds that the
primary extension is rung before any extensions in the follow-me list are rung. This
can be a value between 0 and 60. Setting this to 0 will cause Asterisk to immediately
start ringing the members of the follow-me list instead of trying to ring the primary
extension first. As the primary extension can be included as a member of the follow-
me list, this is often the desired behavior.

The **Ring Strategy** drop-down menu allows the order in which the follow-me list members will be rung to be configured. There are 10 available ring strategies. The ring strategies in a follow-me route are identical to those used in a ring group. Please refer to the *Ring Groups* section of Chapter 5, *Basic Call Targets* for ring strategy definitions.

Ring Time (max 60 sec) configures the maximum number of seconds for which a phone will be rung before the call is considered failed. For hunt ring strategies, this is the number of seconds that each round of the hunt sequence will ring the appropriate phone.

Follow-Me List is the list of extensions that should be rung for this follow-me route. Extensions should be listed one per line. As with ring groups and queues, external numbers and extensions can be listed as long as they are suffixed with a pound (#) symbol. For example, 5551234567#.

The **Extension Quick Pick** drop-down menu lists all previously configured extensions on the system. Selecting an extension from this menu will place that extension into the **Follow-Me List**.

The **Announcement** option is the pre-recorded message that will be played to the caller before any of the Follow-Me List members are rung. This message can serve to inform the caller that several phones are being rung, or to ask them to be patient during the process (for example, "Please wait while the person you are trying to reach is located."). Recordings can be added in the FreePBX **System Recordings** screen (more information on System Recordings can be found in the *Custom Voice Prompts* section of Chapter 9).

The **Play Music On Hold?** drop-down menu allows a selection of the music-on-hold class to be played for the caller while they are waiting for all follow-me list members to be rung. Selecting **None** will play nothing while extensions are tried. Selecting **Ring** will play ringing instead of music on hold. Music classes can be defined in the FreePBX **Music on Hold** screen (more information on Music on Hold can be found in the *Custom Music on Hold* section of Chapter 9).

The **CID Name Prefix** field allows text to be prepended to the caller ID name of all of the callers who pass through this follow-me route.

The **Alert Info** allows custom text to be sent in the SIP ALERT_INFO headers for all calls that pass through this follow-me route. ALERT_INFO headers are often used to force a distinctive ring, or auto-answer on compatible SIP endpoints.

When **Confirm Calls** is enabled, then the person who answers a call from this follow-me route will be prompted to press *1* before the call will be bridged to their endpoint. Requiring the user to confirm the call avoids scenarios in which mobile phones send the call to voicemail, Asterisk counts the call as "answered", and bridges the caller to the mobile voicemail (when the call should be sent to the failover destination instead).

Remote Announce is used to select the message that will be played to the person who picks up a call from this follow-me route if **Confirm Calls** is enabled. This message should inform the person receiving the call that they have an inbound follow-me call and need to press *1* to accept it.

Too-Late Announce is the message played to the person receiving the call if they try to confirm a call (by pressing *1*), but someone else has already answered the call. This message should inform them that the call they were trying to accept has been answered by someone else.

Once the follow-me settings have been configured, select a call target for the call to failover to in the event that none of the listed extensions pick up:

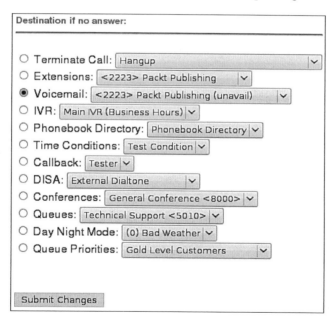

In many cases, the failover destination will be the voicemail for the user account that this follow-me belongs to (but the destination can be any valid call target on the system).

Once all options are configured, click on the **Submit Changes** button and then click on the orange-colored **Apply Configuration Changes** bar at the top of the screen.

VmX Locater

The VmX Locater is a very simplified version of the default FreePBX follow-me setup. These settings can be set and edited by the FreePBX administrator, but if the locater is enabled for a user, then they will be able to change these settings themselves using the Asterisk Recording Interface.

Note that the VmX Locater can work in conjunction with the FreePBX follow-me routing, instead of replacing it entirely. The VmX Locator prompts are played when a caller would normally reach voicemail. At that point, the caller can be directed to press *0* for the operator, *1* to run through follow-me routing, and *2* for an optional additional extension.

To set up the VmX Locater in FreePBX, click on the **Users** or **Extensions** link in the navigation menu under the **Basic** section. The link that is present will depend on the operational mode that FreePBX is running in (DeviceAndUser or Extensions):

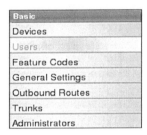

Click on the name of the user that requires VmX Locater configuration and scroll down to the bottom of the page to find the VmX Locater settings:

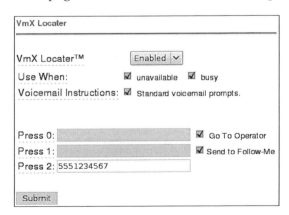

To enable the **VmX Locater**, select **Enabled** in the first drop-down menu.

The **Use When** checkboxes allow the locater to be engaged when the called user is **unavailable, busy**, or both. Note that if neither checkbox is selected, the locater will never be engaged.

The **Voicemail Instructions** checkbox configures whether or not to play the standard Asterisk voicemail prompts after the user's pre-recorded outgoing voicemail message. If this box is not selected, the user's message will be played and will be immediately followed by a beep. Otherwise, the standard prompts asking the caller to "please leave their message after the tone" will be played.

The **Press 0, Press 1**, and **Press 2** fields can be used to configure specific extensions, ring groups, queues, or external phones to be rung when the appropriate digit is pressed during playback of the outgoing voicemail message. When the VmX Locater is enabled, the associated user should re-record their voicemail prompts to ask the user to press one of these three digits, in order to route the call appropriately. External phone numbers used in these fields *do not* require pound symbols at the end of them.

The **Press 0** field can optionally be configured to redirect the caller to the PBX operator (defined on the FreePBX **General Settings** screen) instead of a specific extension or phone number.

The **Press 1** field can optionally be configured to redirect the caller to the default FreePBX follow-me settings for the user (if they have also been configured).

When all settings have been configured, click on the **Submit** button followed by the orange-colored **Apply Configuration Changes** bar to save the changes and make them live.

When the user is logged into the ARI web interface, they can view and edit these settings by clicking on the **VmX Locator** link in the navigation menu:

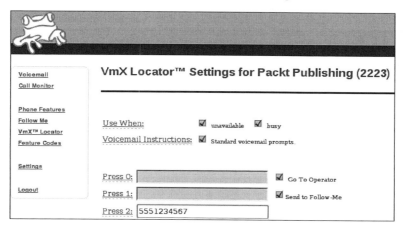

Outbound routing and Least Cost Routing

Outbound routing is a set of rules that FreePBX uses to decide which trunk to use for an outbound call. Many VoIP systems have multiple trunks, and it can often be unnecessarily expensive to route all calls over a single trunk. Outbound routing also allows dialed numbers to be rewritten on the fly (to remove or prepend dialed numbers with specific outside access codes or area codes). Routes are defined using patterns, against which the dialed numbers are matched.

Outbound routes have a priority. If a dialed number matches the pattern in two outbound routes, the route with the lower priority will be used to place the call.

To start setting up an outbound route, click on the **Outbound Routes** link in the navigation menu is under the **Basic** section:

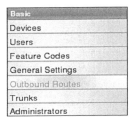

The **Add Route** page consists of eight configurable options and one "quick pick" drop-down menu used to populate certain fields as shown in the following screenshot:

Route Name is just used to identify this route. This value cannot contain any spaces. The name is usually descriptive of the purpose of the route (for example, "local" or "international").

The **Route Password** field can be used to secure a route against unauthorized dialing. For example, a company may wish to restrict all long distance calls, or calls to 1-900 numbers. A numerical password can be placed in this field, or a direct path to a file containing a list of valid passwords (one password per line). When this field is not blank, all calls that pass through this outbound route will not be placed through any provider until the caller successfully enters a valid password.

The **PIN Set** field performs the same function as the **Route Password** field but uses previously created password sets. PIN sets can be configured in the FreePBX **PIN Sets** screen (more information on PIN Sets can be found in the *PIN Sets* section of Chapter 9). If PIN sets will be used, the **Route Password** field must be left blank. If both the **Route Password** field is left blank and the **PIN Set** field is set to **None**, callers will be able to use this route without authentication.

The **Emergency Dialing** checkbox is used to specify that the route will *only* be used for emergency calls. When this option is set, any calls that pass through this route will set their caller ID to the emergency CID setting of the device the call originated from (if set). Do not select this option if the route may sometimes route emergency calls. Only select this option if the route will *always* be used to route emergency calls.

If the **Intra Company Route** option is selected, then the caller ID of the device that initiated the call will be preserved instead of having the caller ID rewritten to whatever is specified by the trunk. This option should be used when an outbound route is directing calls to another VoIP system from the same company, and the call is not passing over public telephony routes.

The **Music On Hold?** drop-down menu allows a specific music-on-hold class to be selected for calls that pass through this outbound route. Once a call is placed through this route, the music that is heard anytime the call is placed on hold will be defined by the class selected in this field.

The **Dial Patterns** field is the heart of every outbound route. Specific numbers can be matched here (for example, 911 or 999). Otherwise, patterns can be specified using the characters in the following table:

Pattern	Description
X	Any whole number from 0-9.
Z	Any whole number from 1-9.
N	Any whole number from 2-9.
[###]	Any whole number in the brackets. Note that multiple numbers can be separate by commas, and ranges of numbers can be specified with a dash ([1, 3, 6-8] would match the numbers 1, 3, 6, 7, and 8).
.	It matches one or more characters (acts as a wildcard).

The **Trunk Sequence** drop-down menus are for configuring the order in which the trunks will be used when calls match the pattern specified in the **Dial Patterns** field. If the first trunk in the list is unavailable or congested, the call will fail over to the second trunk. This behavior will repeat until all listed trunks have been exhausted.

The **Dial patterns wizards** and **Trunk Sequence** fields are where the concept of **Least Cost Routing (LCR)** comes into play. LCR involves configuring each outbound route to send calls to the cheapest trunk first. This often involves setting up multiple outbound routes for similar styles of calls. For example, say that a FreePBX system is configured with two SIP trunks—one from a provider that allows unlimited flat-rate calling to the state of New York and one from a provider that allows unlimited flat-rate calls to the state of California. It seems logical that calls to the New York area codes should be routed via the New York trunk and calls to the California area codes should be routed via the California trunk. However, with a single route to match US-format calls, all calls will prefer a single trunk first and charges will apply when calls could be free. In this case, it would make sense to create two outbound routes.

The first route would have a pattern that would match all calls for New York state area codes (dialed in both local and long-distance formats). The **Trunk Sequence** set of fields would list the New York trunk first and the California trunk second.

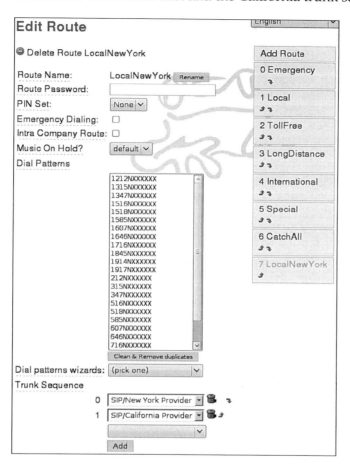

The second route would have a pattern that matches all calls for California state area codes (again, in both local and long distance formats). The **Trunk Sequence** set of fields would be reversed to have the California provider first and the New York provider second:

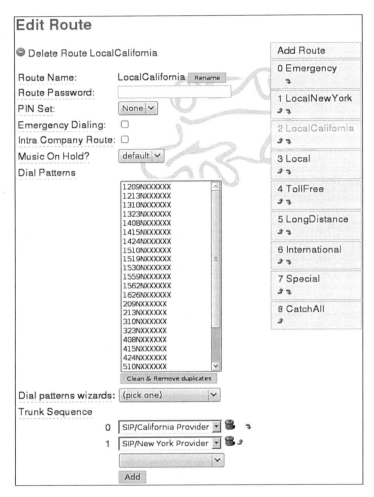

In this manner, when FreePBX routes a call to either New York or California, it will attempt to use the cheapest route first. The end goal is that all users on the system should be able to dial a number just as they normally would, without having to worry about manually picking the cheapest line or dialing the call in a special way. Whenever they dial a number, the PBX is smart enough to dial it properly, using the most economical trunk.

Once trunk options have been configured, click on the **Submit Changes** button followed by the orange-colored **Apply Configuration Changes** bar at the top of the screen to make the new outbound route live.

A note about routes

It is extremely easy to forget about a particular type of call and leave out the associated outbound route. Doing so can leave users stranded when they need to make an important call. Be sure to include methods to dial the following types of calls:

Emergency: Dedicate a route just for this purpose. Calls for emergency services should never be mangled by another dial pattern.

Local: Calls to local numbers (usually NXXXXXXXXX).

Toll-free: Calls to toll-free numbers (such as 1-888 or 1-800 numbers).

International: Calls outside of the country, if permitted (usually 011).

Special: Calls that do not fit any other category. This includes calls such as calls to the operator (0) and directory assistance (411).

Long distance: Calls outside of the local calling area, if permitted (usually 1NXXXXXXXXX).

Summary

By this point, our FreePBX system should be routing calls! This chapter discussed setting up inbound routes to match against the number that was dialed and the number that the caller is dialing from. Inbound calls can also be run against a follow-me route or a VmX Locater route in order to attempt to find a user who is not at their desk phone. Our FreePBX system should also be able to detect and route inbound faxes, should any fax come through our trunks. In addition, outbound calls will now be routed properly using the most economical routes.

The next chapter will discuss taking all those calls that are now running through our system and recording them for playback later.

8
Recording Calls

Asterisk has a wonderful, built-in ability to record calls. No additional software is required to make this happen. When Asterisk records a call, both sides of the call are recorded and written out to a file for playback on a computer. Call recording is often performed in call centers to ensure call quality, or to keep calls for later review, should the need arise. Asterisk provides the ability to record all of the calls, or to selectively record calls.

In this chapter, we will discuss the following:

- General recording options
- Recording calls to extensions
- Recording calls to queues
- Recording calls to conferences
- Maintaining call recordings

Be aware of the call recording laws

Before enabling call recording for your PBX, make sure that you are aware of the legalities surrounding call recordings and privacy laws. Call recordings are prohibited in certain places, unless the caller is told that the call will be recorded. For example, in the state of California all of the parties on the call must consent to the call being recorded before it begins. Playing back a message stating that the call is being recorded prior to the call being answered is considered a valid form of consent.

Recording formats

FreePBX allows calls to be recorded in the following formats:

- WAV
- WAV49
- ULAW
- ALAW
- SLN
- GSM

Each format has its own ratio of file size to recording quality, and certain formats will not play on all of the computers. A comparison between all of the available formats is as follows:

Format	Description
WAV	Uncompressed WAV format recording. Sound quality will be very good, but the file will be very large in size (roughly 1 megabyte per minute of the recording). WAV format recordings are natively playable on nearly all of the computers without additional software.
WAV49	WAV format recorded using the GSM codec. As GSM is a compressed codec, the sound quality is compromised. Sound quality on a GSM recording is usually equivalent to the quality that is achieved during mobile telephone calls. File size is much smaller than a standard WAV (roughly 100 kilobytes per minute of the recording); WAV49 files are often difficult to play on computers without additional software that understands the GSM codec.
ULAW or ALAW	G.711 codec recording. The recording quality is excellent, and should sound exactly like the call did to all of the parties who were on the original call. File size is very large (similar to the WAV format at about 1 megabyte per minute). ULAW and ALAW recordings are very difficult to play on most computers. There are very few computers that will play the recording without additional software that understands the G.711 codec.
SLN	Asterisk native SLINEAR format. Recordings that are in SLN format will have the same quality and file size as WAV recordings. SLN recordings are raw WAV, little endian 16-bit signed linear (PCM) format recordings. Most computers will play these files, although some software packages refuse to play them unless the extension is renamed to .wav from .sln.
GSM	GSM codec recording. As with WAV49 calls, the quality of GSM recordings is less than that of ULAW/ALAW or WAV calls, but is generally acceptable for most purposes. GSM recordings weigh in at around 100 kilobytes per minute.

Transcoding during recording

One very important aspect of call recording to keep in mind is that if the recording uses a different codec than the original call, transcoding must occur. For example, a call that uses the G.711 ULAW codec that is being recorded using the WAV49 format will need to be transcoded into the GSM codec before being saved. Transcoding recordings place additional load on a server's disk I/O and processor resources. On high traffic systems, it is possible to max out all of the available resources if the transcoding recordings are not accounted for.

In general, the rule of thumb for recording will be the same as it is for selecting the codec that a trunk or extension will use: try to make everything match. If all of the calls are using the GSM codec, then it would be safe to record those calls in the GSM format. A system that has all of the calls in G.711 ULAW format would be put under an unnecessary amount of stress to record in GSM format. If transcoding is required (for example, limited disk space dictates the use of GSM recordings), be sure to size the resources of the system accordingly in order to allow the additional load.

General call recording options

FreePBX has several settings that govern the global operation of call recording. These settings determine if call recording should be globally enabled or disabled, which format to record calls in, and a command to run after a call has been recorded (if desired).

In order to access the global options, click on **General Settings** in the navigation menu on the left as shown in the following screenshot:

The **Call Recording** section has the settings that we are interested in:

Call Recording	
Extension Recording Override:	Disabled ∨
Call recording format:	wav ∨
Recording Location:	
Run after record:	

The **Extension Recording Override** option allows all user-level automatic call recording to be disabled. A user can be set up to record all of the calls (which will be discussed shortly). If this option is set to **Enabled**, all of the user settings will be ignored and calls will not be recorded automatically. Note that this option neither affects recording settings for queues or conferences, which can be set up in order to record all of the calls, nor does it affect on-demand recording. This setting only affects users who have been set up to automatically record all of the calls. If this field is set to **Disabled** then the user-level recording options will be respected.

The **Call recording format** field allows us to change the format of the call in which it will be stored. The default value is **wav**, but can be changed to **WAV** (WAV49—a GSM file stored as a **wav**), **ulaw**, **alaw**, **sln**, **gsm**, and **g729**. More information on recording formats can be found earlier in this chapter in the *Recording formats* section.

Recording Location lets us change the default location that recorded files will be stored in. The default location is `/var/spool/asterisk/monitor`. In order to change this location, enter a full file path in this field, including the trailing slash (for example, `/media/callrecordings/`).

Run after record lets us specify a command or script to be run, after a recording has been saved. This script will be run each time any call is recorded. This could be used to move recordings to a new location, delete old recordings, or to notify an administrator that a new recording is available.

Recording calls

FreePBX can be configured in order to record calls to a particular extension, queue, or conference. If a call encounters a request to initiate recording twice (for example, a caller enters a queue that is being recorded and the agent who picks up has set up their extension to record all of the calls), the call will only be recorded once. The call will be recorded by the target that first answered the call. In the previous example, the queue would record the call as the queue answered the call before the extension did.

If a call encounters conflicting recording instructions (for example, a caller enters a queue that is being recorded, but the agent who picks up has set up their extension to never record calls), the call will still be recorded. The target that has recording enabled will record the call. It is important to note that there is no way to stop a call from being recorded if it utilizes a call target that is set up to always record calls.

Recording calls to extensions

FreePBX allows all of the calls to a particular user to be recorded, or for calls to be selectively recorded. FreePBX allows the choice between recording only incoming calls, only outgoing calls, or both.

In order to set up call recording for a particular user, click on **Users** or **Extensions** in the navigation bar on the left (this depends on the operational mode in which FreePBX is running. More information on setting up users/extensions can be found in Chapter 3, *Devices and Extensions*):

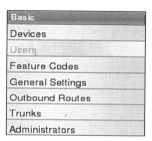

Click on the name of the user you wish to edit and scroll down to the **Recording Options** section:

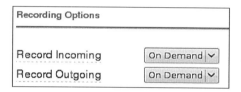

The **Record Incoming** and **Record Outgoing** settings can be configured as **On Demand**, **Always**, or **Never**.

When the **On Demand** option is selected, the user can dial *1 during a call to start recording the call. *1 can be dialed again to stop recording the call. The on demand toggle only lasts for the current call. In order to record the next call, the user would have to dial *1 again.

If these options are set to **Always**, then all of the calls in the selected direction will be recorded. When **Always** is selected, pressing *1 will *not* stop call recording.

If these options are set to **Never**, then no calls in the selected direction will be recorded. When **Never** is selected, pressing *1 will *not* start recording.

Be sure to click on the **Submit** button, followed by the orange-colored **Apply Configuration Changes** bar at the top of the screen in order to save any changes made to the recording settings.

Recording calls to queues

All the calls to a particular queue can be recorded. This is often used on larger call queues for later call review by management, or to resolve disputes about what was said on a particular call. In order to record all of the calls that are picked up out of a particular queue, click on the **Queues** link under the **Inbound Call Control** menu on the left as shown in the following screenshot:

Click on the name of the queue in the menu on the right, which needs call recording enabled:

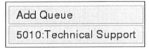

Under **Queue Options**, the **Call Recording** drop-down menu can be changed to **wav49**, **wav**, and **gsm**.

Queue Options	
Agent Announcement:	None
Join Announcement:	None
Music on Hold Class:	inherit
Ringing Instead of MoH:	☐
Max Wait Time:	Unlimited
Max Callers:	0
Join Empty:	Yes
Leave When Empty:	No
Ring Strategy:	ringall
Agent Timeout:	15 seconds
Retry:	5 seconds
Wrap-Up-Time:	0 seconds
Call Recording:	wav
Event When Called:	No
Member Status:	No
Skip Busy Agents:	No
Queue Weight:	0
Autofill:	☐
Agent Regex Filter	

Select the desired recording format, click on the **Submit Changes** button, and click on the orange-colored **Apply Configuration Changes** bar in order to enable recording on the queue.

Note that queues tend to have a high volume of calls. It is important to select an appropriate call recording format, and to ensure that recordings are maintained and cleaned up periodically. More information on recording formats can be found earlier in the *Recording formats* section of this chapter. Recording maintenance is discussed later in this chapter in the *Maintaining call recordings* section.

Recording calls to conferences

All of the calls to a particular conference room can be recorded. All of the members of the conference will be recorded and merged into a single file. In order to enable call recordings for a particular conference, select **Conferences** from the **Internal Options & Configuration** menu on the left as shown in the following screenshot:

Select the conference room that should have recording enabled from the menu on the right:

Under **Conference Options**, the **Record Conference** drop-down menu will turn recording on or off:

Selecting **Yes** will record the entire conference (from the time the first member joins) in WAV format (more information on the WAV format can be found earlier in this chapter in the *Recording formats* section). Selecting a different format to record the conference in is not currently supported. Once **Yes** has been selected from the **Record Conference** drop-down menu, click on the **Submit Changes** button followed by the orange-colored **Apply Configuration Changes** button in order to enable call recordings for the conference.

Maintaining call recordings

It is worth noting that call recordings can be quite large. If left unattended, a PBX that automatically records all of the calls will eventually fill up the entire available hard disk space and stop processing calls. It is important to have a maintenance strategy for dealing with call recordings in order to avoid this. While third-party tools exist to maintain recordings, adequate maintenance can often be performed with simple shell scripts.

The most common way of maintaining call recordings is to automate the deletion of recordings that are older than a certain time frame. The following script called `OldRecordingDeletion.sh` will remove all of the recordings older than 14 days.

```bash
#!/bin/bash

# Change this path to reflect your recording storage
# location
RECORDINGS=/var/spool/asterisk/monitor

# Change this number to reflect the maximum age of call
# recordings
RECORDINGEXPIRY=14

# Change this number to reflect the maximum age of the
# deletion logs
LOGEXPIRY=365

# Current date
DATE=`date`

# Delete recordings older than $EXPIRY days
find $RECORDINGS -mtime +$EXPIRY -exec rm -rfv > removal-$DATE.log\

# Delete log files older than $LOGEXPRY
find . -mtime +$LOGEXPIRY -exec rm -rf\
```

It is best to run a script like this once a day. Adding the following line to cron will execute the script from the /etc/recordingdeletion file once daily at 5:00 a.m.:

```
0 5 * * * /etc/recordingdeletion/OldRecordingDeletion.sh
```

More information on using the cron system can be found later in this chapter in the *Using cron* section.

Another possible method of maintaining recordings is to find the longest calls, and only keep them (since the longer calls are often the calls that prove problematic). The script below (SmallRecordingDeletion.sh) will delete all of the recordings under 15 MB.

The following script is written for maintaining recordings of a single format, and defaults to removing recordings that are less than 15 megabytes in size. This is equivalent to about 15 minutes of calls that are recorded in WAV, ULAW, ALAW, or SLN format. For WAV49 or GSM formats, recordings in a 15 megabyte file would contain over two hours of call time. For these formats, the equivalent value for 15 minutes of talk time is about 1.5 megabytes. If recordings are in multiple formats (for example, queues are recorded in GSM format while conferences are in WAV format), the script would need to be modified to only remove a specific format.

```
#!/bin/bash

# Change this path to reflect your recording storage
# location
RECORDINGS=/var/spool/asterisk/monitor

# Change this number to reflect the minimum size of
# recordings
RECORDINGSIZE=15

# Change this number to reflect the maximum age of the
# deletion logs
LOGEXPIRY=365

# Current date
DATE=`date`

# Delete recordings older than $EXPIRY days
find $RECORDINGS  -size -$RECORDINGSIZE M -exec rm -rfv > removal-
$DATE.log\

# Delete log files older than $LOGEXPRY
find . -mtime +$LOGEXPIRY -exec rm -rf\
```

This script should also be run once per day. Adding the following line to cron will execute the script from `/etc/recordingdeletion` once daily at 5:00 a.m.:

```
0 5 * * * /etc/recordingdeletion/SmallRecordingDeletion.sh
```

Using cron

The cron system allows scheduled executions of any command that can be run from the server's command line. The easiest way to add an entry to cron is to edit the `crontab` file using the following command:

```
crontab -e
```

If the `crontab` file has not been edited previously, crontab manager may ask which editor to use by providing a numbered list such as the one below:

```
Select an editor.  To change later, run 'select-editor'.
  1. /usr/bin/vim.tiny
  2. /bin/ed
  3. /bin/nano        <---- easiest
```

Press the number that corresponds with the desired editor and then press the *Enter* key. If `crontab` has not previously been used, then a blank text file will be opened for editing. If the file has previously been edited, then all of the existing entries will be shown in the text editor.

In order to add a new entry to the file, simply place your cursor at the end of the file (below all other text) and start typing. A crontab entry should use the following syntax: `(min) (hour) (day) (month) (dayofweek) (command)`. Each token can be replaced as follows:

- `(min)` can be replaced with the minute when the command should be run. For example, if the command is to be run at 2:30 a.m., enter `30` for the minute. Valid values are any whole numbers between zero and 59.

- `(hour)` should be replaced with the hour when the command should be run. For the previous example, running a command at 2:30 a.m. would replace `(hour)` with `2`. Valid values are any whole numbers between zero and 23.

- `(day)` should be replaced with the day of the month that the command should be run on. For example, to run a command on July 20th, enter `20`. Valid values are whole numbers between one and 31. Note that the system will not generate an error if the entered date does not exist (for example, entering a cron job to run on September 31st will not generate an error). If an invalid date is entered, the command will never run.

- (month) should be replaced with the number corresponding to the month that the command is to be run in. For example, to run the command on July 20 enter 7 (because July is the seventh month). Valid values are whole numbers between one and 12.

- (dayofweek) should be replaced with the number corresponding to the day of the week that the command should be run on. For example, to run a command on a Thursday, enter 4 (because counting from Sunday as day zero, Thursday is the fourth day of the week). Valid values are whole numbers between zero and seven. Sunday can either be zero or seven, cron will recognize both.

- (command) should be replaced with the shell command that is being run. As cron does not run under a particular shell, it has no environment variables and does not know the path to various system executables. The full path to a command must be entered. For example, in order to reboot the system each time the cron job is executed, the command would be /sbin/reboot now.

For any of the timing values (minute, hour, day, month, or day of week), an asterisk (*) can be used to represent all of the possible values. For example, the following cron entry would reload Asterisk's configuration on the fifteenth minute of every hour:

```
15 * * * * /usr/sbin/asterisk -rx "reload"
```

A range of values can also be specified in order to execute a command within a specific time frame. For example, the cron entry below would reload Asterisk's configuration once on the fifteenth minute of every hour, but only on business days:

```
15 * * * 1-5 /usr/sbin/asterisk -rx "reload"
```

It is also possible to specify a set of values using a comma (,). For example, the cron entry below would reload Asterisk's configuration once per hour on the fifteenth minute of the hour, only during business hours (excluding lunch hour), and only on business days:

```
15 9,10,11,13,14,15,16,17 * * 1-5 /usr/sbin/asterisk -rx "reload"
```

 The previous entries are a single cron entry and should be typed on a single line.

Finally, the forward slash (/) can be used to specify what is known as "step values". Step values allow a command to be run a fraction of the amount of times it would be normally within a given time frame. For example, specifying `9-17/2` for the hour field would execute the command every two hours between the hours of 9:00 a.m. and 5:00 p.m. instead of once per hour during that time frame. The following cron entry would reboot the server on the first day of every third month at 2:00 a.m.:

```
0 2 * */3 * /sbin/reboot now
```

Once the entry has been completed, save the file and close the text editor (the method to accomplish this is different based on which editor is being used). A message will be displayed indicating that the `cron` file has been updated with a new version:

```
crontab: installing new crontab
```

The schedule for cron entries can be changed any time by reopening the `crontab` file for editing.

Summary

By now, we have learned how to record any call that enters our PBX, if we choose to do so. We now know of the importance of maintaining our recordings so that they do not fill up the hard disk on our PBX, and we are able to create some basic scripts to accomplish recording maintenance (with a little help from cron).

The next chapter will focus on personalizing our PBX by changing the default music on hold, recording custom voice prompts, and customizing feature codes/star codes.

Personalizing Your PBX *9*

After all that hard work, we finally have a working PBX. It's time to make the PBX our own. FreePBX allows for several options to customize the way our call structures sound. In this chapter, we will discuss how to:

- Upload our own custom music that will be played when callers are placed on hold
- Record custom voice prompts to answer incoming calls automatically
- Customize star codes that users will dial to activate various features
- Set up automated callback systems
- Configure **Direct Inward System Access (DISA)** to give remote agents a dial tone, no matter what phone they call in from
- Configure customer caller ID lookup sources to properly identify incoming callers
- Configure PIN sets for increased security
- Configure custom applications
- Configure custom destinations

Custom Music on Hold

FreePBX allows two styles of music-on-hold customization—static files and streaming. Static files are audio files (such as WAV or MP3 files) that are uploaded to the FreePBX server and played back when a caller is placed on hold. Streaming audio is used to connect to a live audio feed from a particular source. Typically, this would be an Internet stream (many radio stations broadcast over the Internet), but it could also be a stream from a sound card or some other audio device.

FreePBX separates different groups of music on hold into categories. Different static file categories can contain different sets of files. Each streaming category can only contain one audio stream. Music-on-hold categories can be applied to inbound routes (so that all calls that match the route will hear that category) as well as to queues and ring groups. Categories assigned at the call target level will override the music-on-hold category for that particular target only. Once a call leaves that target it will fall back into the music-on-hold category specified in the inbound route, which it was matched against.

Using audio files for Music on Hold

In order to create a music-on-hold category using static audio files, click on the **Music on Hold** link under the **Internal Options & Configuration** menu on the left:

Click on the **Add Music Category** link in the menu on the right:

The initial setup screen for a static file category has one only field as shown in the following screenshot:

Type a name for the category in the textbox and click on the **Submit Changes** button. On the resulting screen, click on the **Browse** button to find an MP3 or WAV file for upload, and then click on the **Upload** button. The quality of the files is not terribly important, as FreePBX will downsample everything it gets to mono 8 kHz, 8 bits-per-sample, ULAW format.

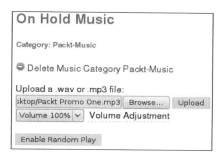

After clicking on the **Upload** button, FreePBX will display a warning as shown in the following screenshot:

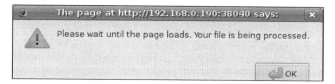

 Make sure that this warning is followed. After you click on the **OK** button, the page will still be loading. With larger files or slower connections, it can take several minutes for the page to load. Navigating to a new page before the page has finished loading will result in an incomplete upload and a corrupted music-on-hold file that will not function correctly.

Once the page has finished loading, the music file that was uploaded will be present as shown in the following screenshot:

The music category is now ready for use (although it will only have one music file in it that will be played over and over again). Repeat the upload process for as many additional files as you would want to add. Music files will be played in the order in which they are uploaded unless random play is enabled. By clicking on the **Enable Random Play** button, the songs are played to the caller in a random order.

Using audio streams for Music on Hold

Using an audio stream for music on hold is a bit more complicated than using static audio files, and the results can be somewhat unpredictable depending on the source and type of the stream. Nonetheless, it is definitely possible to set up a live stream as a music-on-hold category. The only restriction Asterisk imposes on the music stream is that it must be a mono 8 kHz, 8 bits-per-sample, ULAW audio stream. Most streaming audio programs support converting their streams to a new output format on the fly.

A streaming music-on-hold class can negatively affect the performance of a PBX due to bandwidth usage or transcoding issues. Each streaming class should be streamed only once at any given time (if multiple callers are placed on hold, all of them will be connected to the same stream). However, if multiple streaming classes are created, it is possible for multiple streams to be active at the same time. Each active stream can take up a significant amount of bandwidth (standard online broadcasts usually run at the speed of 96 kbps or 128 kbps). It is important to take bandwidth usage into account when planning a system. Five different streaming classes active at the same time could take up one-third of the available downstream bandwidth of a T1 line.

In addition to bandwidth issues, a streaming music-on-hold class may require transcoding to be played to a caller. Asterisk requires that the a stream be in ULAW format, so calls already using the G.711 ULAW codec will be able to listen to the stream without any transcoding. A call that is using a compressed codec such as G.729 would force the stream to be transcoded for the caller to hear it. Not only does this place additional processing load on the PBX, but it also requires an additional G.729 license for the concurrent caller that the stream has to be transcoded for. If there are few processor resources available or the available codec licensing will be a problem, it may be beneficial to avoid streaming music on hold all together.

To set up a streaming music-on-hold category, click on the **Music on Hold** link under the **Internal Options & Configuration** menu on the left as shown in the following screenshot:

Click on the **Add Streaming Category** link in the menu on the right as shown in the following screenshot:

The streaming category setup screen has three fields as shown in the following screenshot:

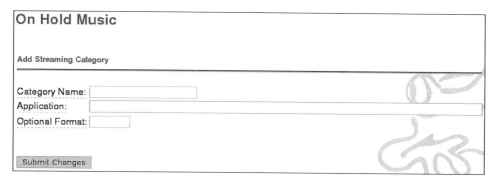

The **Category Name** is a name for the streaming class, which will be used as a reference to the stream when selecting it wherever it is used in your call trees.

The **Application** field is likely to be the most complicated one that FreePBX asks for. The value in this field is the program or script that Asterisk will invoke in order to start "listening" to the stream. For RAW TCP streams, the built-in streamplayer application can be used in the format of /usr/sbin/streamplayer server port. However, this will only work for RAW TCP streams, and will not play icecast or shoutcast streams.

In order to play icecast or shoutcast streams, a shell script is typically written, which is invoked by Asterisk. The shell script will use a combination of various audio programs to start the stream, convert it to an acceptable format, and then feed it to Asterisk. For example, the following script called streamicecast.sh uses ogg123 to start a stream from icecastserver.net and uses sox to convert the stream to the required format:

```
#!/bin/bash

# /usr/bin/streamicecast.sh

# Streams icecast feed from icecastserver.net for use

# with Asterisk and FreePBX

/usr/bin/ogg123 -q -b 128 -p 32 -d wav -f - http://icecastserver.net/
| sox -r 16000 -t wav - -r 8000 -c 1 -t raw - vol 0.25
```

Then, we would just simply have to put /usr/bin/streamicecast.sh in the **Application** field.

The **Optional Format** field is used to tell Asterisk the format of the stream. This must be a format that Asterisk understands (such as ULAW or GSM). For the most part, it is safest to leave this field blank and force the stream to the proper ULAW format.

Click on the **Submit Changes** button to save the stream for use in inbound routes, ring groups, and queues.

Custom voice prompts

Voice prompts are played to a caller when the caller enters an IVR, a follow-me, a ring group, or anywhere else they might be prompted for input. The purpose of a prompt is to instruct the user what to do. This is usually something as simple as, "Thank you for calling Packt Publishing. Press *1* for sales, *2* for publishing, or an extension at any time."

Recording custom voice prompts

FreePBX provides a simple method for recording new voice prompts right from a telephone handset.

To record a new script, click on the **System Recordings** link under the **Internal Options & Configuration** menu on the left as shown in the following screenshot:

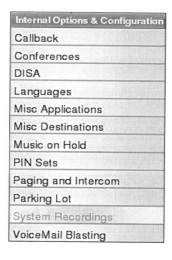

Click on the **Add Recording** link in the menu on the right as shown in the following screenshot:

The **Add Recording** screen provides two methods to add system recordings to FreePBX:

- Uploading existing audio files
- Recording new audio files via a VoIP endpoint

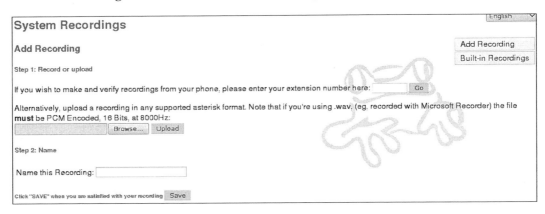

Uploading an existing recording is done in the same way in which a static music file is uploaded to a music-on-hold category (click on the **Browse** button, select the desired file, and click on the **Upload** button).

To record a new prompt, enter the extension of the endpoint you will be recording from into the extension number box and click on the **Go** button. The screen will change to reflect that an extension has been entered:

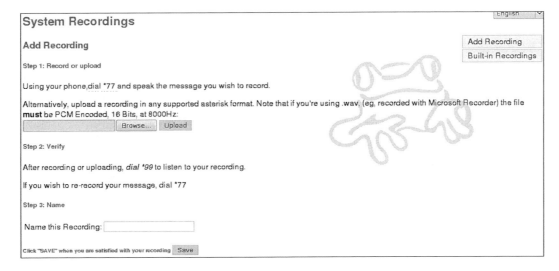

In order to record a new prompt, dial *77 on the extension that was entered and begin speaking after the beep. Hang up when recording is complete. To review the recording, dial *99 from the extension that was entered. Repeat this process until you are satisfied with the recording.

Enter a name for the recording in the **Name this Recording** box. Note that the name can only contain letters and numbers, not spaces and special characters (for example, the characters that may not be used include ", -, +, =, *, &, ^, %, $, #, @, !).

Click on the **Save** button when you have finished recording. The recording will show up in the menu on the right.

Merging existing voice prompts

FreePBX also allows existing voice prompts to be merged together. A merged prompt will be played as a single, continuous file. To merge prompts, click on the **System Recordings** link under the **Internal Options & Configuration** menu on the left:

Internal Options & Configuration
Callback
Conferences
DISA
Languages
Misc Applications
Misc Destinations
Music on Hold
PIN Sets
Paging and Intercom
Parking Lot
System Recordings
VoiceMail Blasting

Click on the **Built-in Recordings** link in the menu on the right as shown in the following screenshot:

The **Built-in Recordings** screen has a single drop-down menu. Select the recording you wish to start with as the base recording from this menu, and click on the **Go** button as shown in the following screenshot:

The **Edit Recording** screen will be shown as follows:

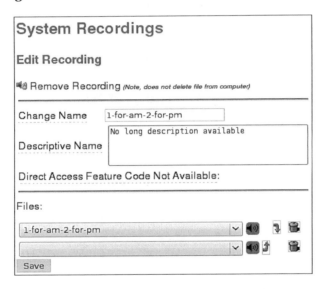

The **Change Name** field changes the name of the recording. The name should be changed to distinguish the merged recording with the original recording.

The value of the **Descriptive Name** field is displayed as a hint to what the recording contains when it is being selected in places such as queues and IVRs.

The **Files** drop-down menus are where individual recordings are selected to be merged. Select a recording from the second drop-down menu and click on the **Save** button to add it to the merged recording. This can be done many times to include several recordings as shown in the following screenshot:

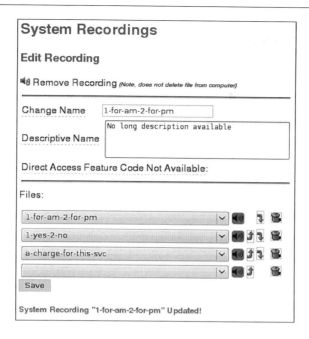

Clicking on the arrow buttons will move a recording up or down, changing the order in which it will be played, and clicking on the garbage buttons will remove a recording from the merged recording.

You must make sure to click on the **Save** button after making any of the changes.

Directory search options

Most PBX systems provide a directory search option that allows callers to enter the first few letters of a person's name to determine their extension. As long as a user has a voicemail box, the user will be listed in the directory. FreePBX allows the directory search experience to be customized to taste.

To customize directory search options, click on the **General Settings** link under the **Basic** menu on the left as shown in the following screenshot:

Scroll down to the **Company Directory** section to find the directory search options:

Company Directory	
Find users in the Company Directory by:	first or last name ☑
Announce Extension:	☑
Operator Extension:	2223

The **Find users in the Company Directory by** drop-down menu allows searches to be restricted to the user's first name, last name, or both first name and last name.

If **Announce Extension** is checked, then the extension number of the user being searched for will be played to the caller before the caller is transferred.

The **Operator Extension** is the extension, external phone number, ring group, or queue number that the caller will be transferred to if they press 0 while searching the directory. This is typically used as a fallback in case the caller cannot locate the user they are searching for.

Once these settings have been configured, scroll down to the bottom of the page and click on the **Submit Changes** button.

Customizing feature codes

Feature codes are three-digit extensions that users can dial to enable or disable certain features for themselves. Feature codes are typically prefixed with an asterisk (*) sign followed by two numbers. The feature codes on a FreePBX system can be altered to use a different extension or disabled.

To customize feature codes, click on the **Feature Codes** link under the **Basic** menu on the left as shown in the following screenshot:

All the available features codes will be displayed as shown in the following screenshot:

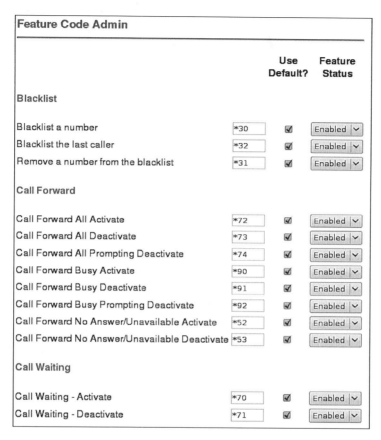

To change the extension that a feature code uses, uncheck the **Use Default?** option and type in the new extension that should be used as shown in the following screenshot:

To disable a feature code entirely, change the drop-down value from **Enabled** to **Disabled** as shown in the following screenshot:

Once the customizations are complete, scroll down to the bottom and click on the **Submit Changes** button to save them.

Callback

A **callback** is a call target that will immediately hang up on a caller, call them back, and then redirect the call to another call target. This is most often used to avoid long-distance charges for remote agents who do not have access to a VoIP endpoint. This is especially relevant in the case of mobile phones where incoming calls are usually significantly cheaper than outgoing calls. The callback target may connect the caller with any resource on the PBX (such as an extension, the voicemail messaging center, or a queue), or it may be used in conjunction with DISA to give the caller a dial tone on the system from which they can call any telephone number they wish (more information on DISA is available later in this chapter in the *Direct Inward System Access (DISA)* section).

In order to set up a callback target, click on the **Callback** option under the **Internal Options & Configuration** section of the navigation menu on the left side of the FreePBX interface as shown in the following screenshot:

Callback targets have only four configuration options:

1. **Callback Description**
2. **Callback Number**
3. **Delay Before Callback**
4. **Destination after Callback**

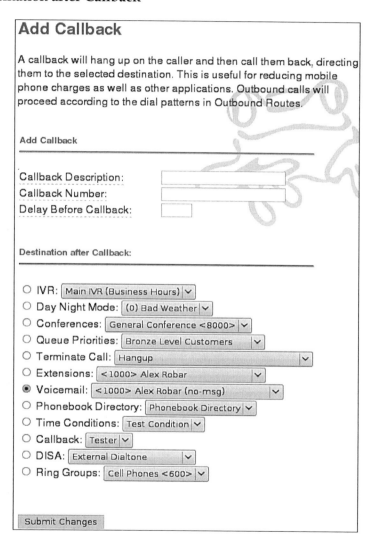

The **Callback Description** field is used to set a name to refer to this callback configuration whenever call targets are being selected in our call trees.

The **Callback Number** field is the telephone number that FreePBX will dial to reconnect with the caller after the call that initiated the callback is terminated. The number must be in a format that one of the outbound routes configured in the **Outbound Routes** section of FreePBX can be matched with (for example, if there is no outbound route defined to match a 10-digit dialing pattern, entering *5551234567* for this field would render the callback configuration useless, as the outbound callback would never be completed). If the field is left blank, then FreePBX will attempt to call back the caller ID number that initiated the callback.

Be sure to test the callback module thoroughly if the Callback Number field is being left blank. Many mobile phones have their caller ID show up as "unknown" or "unavailable" when calls are placed to landline telephone services. If a caller with an unknown caller ID number initiates a callback, the callback will silently fail without any notification to the caller. If there is no way for a caller to send caller ID information, then a callback target will only be useful to that person if it calls them back at a specific predefined telephone number.

Entering a number into the **Delay Before Callback** field will delay the start of the callback process for the number of seconds specified in the field once a callback is initiated. This field is optional and may be left blank if no delay is desired. Certain phone services can take several seconds to be available again after a call is terminated. It is often useful to configure a delay of a few seconds in order to mitigate the risk of the callback module receiving a busy signal while the original caller's service resets itself to accept incoming calls again.

The **Destination after Callback** field is used to configure the call target that the caller will be connected to, once the callback module reconnects the caller to the PBX. Any existing call target is available.

Once all options have been configured, click on the **Submit Changes** button followed by the orange-colored **Apply Configuration Changes** bar to save the callback target and make it active.

A few common examples of when a callback target might be used are as follows:

- A company where employees need the ability to check their voicemail from anywhere. Calling the toll-free company phone number costs the company too much money. A callback target could be set up to call back the incoming caller ID, and be directed to the miscellaneous destination of *98 (more information on **Misc Destinations** can be found later in this chapter in the *Misc Destinations* section). Callers would receive a call on the number they called from, would be prompted for their extension and their password, and would then have access to their voicemail messages.

- A company receives better per-minute rates on calls made through its VoIP trunks than calls made through employees' mobile phones. Employees' mobile phones have free incoming calls. A callback target could be set up for each employee with a mobile phone to call back the employee's mobile number. The callback would be directed to a DISA destination to give the employee a dial tone on the PBX (allowing them to dial out using the company's VoIP trunks without using any outgoing mobile minutes). More information on DISA is available later in this chapter in the *Direct Inward System Access (DISA)* section.

- A company that receives collect calls from anywhere in the world (such as a credit card company that needs to receive calls if a customer's card is lost or stolen). The company reduces their costs if they use a VoIP trunk local to the country that the customer is in, rather than paying for the entire collect call at hefty international rates. A callback target could be set up to call back the incoming caller ID of the customer and be directed to a queue. The customer would receive a call to the number they called from and would be connected with a company representative as soon as one is available.

Direct Inward System Access (DISA)

A DISA call target will provide a caller with a dial tone on the PBX. Once the caller has a dial tone, they can utilize the same set of functions that are utilized by a user with VoIP endpoint attached to the PBX. This means that a person who is remotely located could be given access to dial any extension directly, check their voicemail messages, or even place calls to external telephone numbers through the PBX.

In order to set up a DISA call target, click on the DISA option under the **Internal Options & Configurations** section of the navigation menu on the left side of the FreePBX interface as shown in the following screenshot:

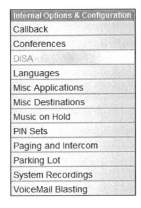

DISA call targets have following eight configuration options:

1. **DISA name**
2. **PIN**
3. **Response Timeout**
4. **Digit Timeout**
5. **Require Confirmation**
6. **Caller ID**
7. **Context**
8. **Allow Hangup**

The **DISA name** field is used to identify the DISA configuration when it is being selected as a call target in other parts of the FreePBX interface.

PIN is used to authenticate a caller when they reach the DISA call target. If the PIN field is not left blank, then the caller will be prompted to enter their authentication code. The PIN that the user enters must match with the value of the PIN field, otherwise the call will be disconnected and the caller will not be able to access the DISA call target. Multiple PIN values can be entered by separating valid PIN values by commas (for example, entering 1234, 5678, 9012 would authenticate callers if they entered any one of the numbers—1234, 5678, 9012 as their PIN when prompted).

The **Response Timeout** field is used to specify how long FreePBX will wait for valid input before disconnecting the call. This not only applies when a caller has not entered any digit yet, but also if a caller has partially entered a number to call without finishing the entry. The default value for this field is 10 seconds, but this is often too short and a caller may feel rushed with this timeout. A setting of 15 or 20 seconds is usually sufficient to allow callers time to enter their desired telephone number without wasting too much time on a dropped call.

The **Digit Timeout** field is used to specify how long FreePBX will wait between digits before dialing the call. If a caller begins entering digits and then stops, FreePBX will wait for however many ever seconds specified in this field, before sending the entered digits to Asterisk for dialing. The default value for this field is five seconds. This is usually sufficient as most people do not take more than five seconds between button pushes on their phone once they have started dialing.

If the **Require Confirmation** option is checked, then FreePBX will prompt the caller to press 1, in order to initiate the DISA process as soon as they are transferred to the DISA call target. If the user fails to press 1, then the call is disconnected. This is useful when calls are transferred directly to a DISA call target through an inbound route that matches the caller ID. It is common for the call to be set up and answered so quickly that the caller will not hear any ring or confirmation before being placed into the DISA call target, and the caller will then time out and disconnect before they realize what happened. Requiring confirmation alerts the user that they are about to enter the DISA call target and allows them to press 1 when they are ready.

The **Caller ID** field is used to set the outbound caller ID of any of the calls that are placed from within the DISA call target. The desired caller ID should be specified in the format of `"Caller Name" <##########>`—`Caller Name` is replaced with the name that should be set on outbound calls and `##########` should be replaced with the phone number that should be set on outbound calls (for example, `"Packt Publishing" <5551234567>`). This is an optional field. If this field is left blank, then the caller ID of the person placing the call will be used.

Setting a caller ID value in the **Caller ID** field does not guarantee that the specified value will be used. If the trunk that routes the call has the **Never Override CallerID** option enabled, then the caller ID will be whatever is specified in the trunk configuration. More information on trunk caller ID options can be found in the *Setting up a New Trunk* section of Chapter 4, *Trunks*.

The **Context** field is used to specify the context in which Asterisk will place the caller when they enter the DISA call target. The context that a user is in defines the features and trunks they have access to. FreePBX places all users into the `from-internal` context by default. As DISA is meant to mimic the functions of an internal user, FreePBX sets the **Context** field to `from-internal` by default as well. Changing this field will require an understanding of the Asterisk configuration files, and will likely mean that a custom context has been manually created in the `/etc/asterisk/extensions_custom.conf` file. Setting a different context in this field could render the DISA call target useless, hence be sure that the context entered here is valid.

If the **Allow Hangup** checkbox is selected, then the caller can press the hangup feature code (by default this code is ******) to end their current call and be presented with a dial tone again. This prevents the caller from actually hanging up their phone, calling back into the PBX, and re-authenticating to gain DISA again. If desired, the feature code for hanging up a call can be changed. More information on how to change the feature codes can be found in the *Customizing Feature Codes* section of this chapter.

Once all options have been configured, click on the **Submit Changes** button followed by the orange-colored **Apply Configuration Changes** bar to save the DISA call target and make it active.

CallerID Lookup Sources

Caller ID lookup sources supplement the caller ID name information that is sent by most telephone companies. A caller ID lookup source contains a list of phone numbers matched with names. When FreePBX receives a call, it can query a lookup source with the number of the caller. If the caller is on the lookup source's list, a name is returned that will be sent along with the call wherever the call gets routed to. The name will be visible on a phone's caller ID display (if the phone supports caller ID), and is also visible in the FreePBX call detail records.

In order to set up a caller ID lookup source, click on the **CallerID Lookup Sources** link under the **Inbound Call Control** section of the navigation menu on the left side of the FreePBX interface as shown in the following screenshot:

The **Add Source** screen has three common configuration options:

1. **Source Description**
2. **Source type**
3. **Cache results**

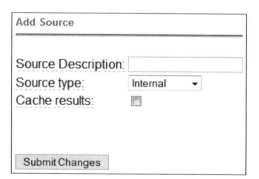

Source Description is used to identify this lookup source when it is being selected as a caller ID lookup source during the configuration of an inbound route.

Source type is used to select the method that this source will use to obtain caller ID name information. FreePBX allows a lookup source to use one of the following methods:

ENUM: FreePBX will use whichever ENUM servers are configured in /etc/asterisk/enum.conf to return caller ID name information. By default, this file contains the e164.arpa and e164.org zones for lookups. All ENUM servers in the enum.conf file will be queried.

- **HTTP**: FreePBX will query a web service for caller ID name information using the HTTP protocol. A lookup source that uses HTTP to query for information can use services such as Google Phonebook or online versions of the white/yellow pages to return caller ID names. When HTTP is selected as the source type, six additional options will appear for configuration. These options are discussed in the *HTTP source type* section.

- **MySQL**: FreePBX will connect to a MySQL database to query for caller ID name information. Usually, this will be a database belonging to a **Customer Relationship Management (CRM)** software package in which all customer information is stored. When MySQL is selected as the Source type, five additional options will appear for configuration. These options are discussed later in the *MySQL source type* section.

- **SugarCRM**: As of FreePBX version 2.5.1, this option is not yet implemented. In the future, this Source type option will allow FreePBX to connect to the database used by the SugarCRM software package to query for caller ID name information.

If the **Cache results** checkbox is selected, then when a lookup source returns results they will be cached in the local AstDB database for quicker retrieval the next time the same number is looked up. Note that values cached in the AstDB will persist past a restart of Asterisk and a reboot of the PBX. Once a caller ID name has been cached, FreePBX will always return that name even if the name in the lookup source changes. Caching must be disabled for a new caller ID name to be returned from the lookup source.

Once all configuration options have been filled out, click on the **Submit Changes** button followed by the orange-colored **Apply Configuration Changes** bar to make the new lookup source available to inbound routes. Now that we have an available lookup source, we can configure an inbound route to use this source to set caller ID information. Click on the **Inbound Routes** link under the **Inbound Call Control** section of the navigation menu on the left side of the FreePBX interface as shown in the following screenshot:

Click the name of the inbound route that will use the new lookup source in the menu on the right side of the page (in this example, **DID 5551234567**) as shown in the following screenshot:

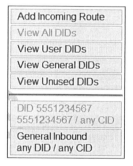

Scroll down the page to the **CID Lookup Source** section. Select the name of the new lookup source from the **Source** drop-down menu:

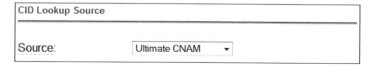

Click on the **Submit** button at the bottom of the page, followed by the orange-colored **Apply Configuration Changes** bar at the top of the page. Calls that are routing using this inbound route will now query our new lookup source for caller ID name information.

HTTP source type

When HTTP is selected as the **Source type** for a caller ID lookup source, six additional configuration options become visible:

1. **Host**
2. **Port**
3. **Username**
4. **Password**
5. **Path**
6. **Query**

```
HTTP

Host:        [                    ]
Port:        [                    ]
Username:    [                    ]
Password:    [                    ]
Path:        [                    ]
Query:       [                    ]
```

The **Host** field is used to specify the hostname or IP address of the web server that hosts the caller ID lookup service. This might be in the format of `server.company.com` or `255.255.255.255`. Only the server hostname or IP address should be entered in this field. Do not include any prefixes or the remainder of the service path here (for example, exclude text such as "http://" and "/lookup.php"). If the service host provided an example address along the lines of `http://server.company.com/lookup.php?q=[number]`, then `server.company.com` would be the value that is entered into the Host field.

The **Port** field is used if the web service is hosted on a custom port. If this field is left blank, then the default value of 80 will be used (most HTTP servers are running on port 80). If the example address supplied by the provider starts with HTTPS instead of HTTP, then enter **443** into the Port field. If the example address has a number after the hostname (for example, `http://server.company.com:8080`), then enter that number into the Port field.

The **Username** and **Password** fields should only be filled in if the service provider supplied a set of credentials to use. If credentials are listed in the sample address supplied by the provider (for example, `http://server.company.com/lookup.php ?q=[number]&username=exampleuser&password=examplepassword`), then do not enter the credentials in these fields. Credentials that are embedded in the web service address will be entered as part of the **Query** field.

The **Path** field is used to specify the path on the web server to the caller ID lookup script. This means everything after the hostname through to the question mark in the service address. For example, if the provider has supplied a service address of `http://server.company.com/callerid/lookup.php?q=[number]`, then `/callerid/lookup.php` is the value that should be entered into the **Path** field. Be sure to include the slash (/) at the beginning of the path.

The **Query** field is the query string that is sent to the web service. The query string is everything that comes after the question mark in the service address. For example, if the provider has supplied a service address of `http://server.company.com/ lookup.php?q=[number]&type=callerid`, then `q=[number]&type=callerid` is the value that should be entered into the **Query** field. The query string must contain a placeholder for the telephone number that is being looked up. FreePBX will replace the special token `[NUMBER]` with the telephone number to look up. If the example address supplied by the provider uses a different token (such as `#NUMBER#`, or `{TelNumber}`), be sure to replace this token with `[NUMBER]`, so that FreePBX will know how to query the provider properly.

A very good example of a free, public HTTP lookup source is the "CallerID Superfecta" script from Nerd Vittles. The script uses an HTTP lookup source to query several public phone books, including:

- Google Phonebook
- AnyWho
- Whitepages

More information on the CallerID Superfecta script can be found at: `http://bestof.nerdvittles.com/applications/callerid/`.

MySQL source type

When MySQL is selected as the Source type for a caller ID lookup source, five additional configuration options become visible:

1. **Host**
2. **Database**
3. **Query**
4. **Username**
5. **Password**

MySQL	
Host:	
Database:	
Query:	
Username:	
Password:	

The **Host** field is used to specify the hostname or IP address of the server that hosts the MySQL database. This might be in the format of `server.company.com`, or `255.255.255.255`. If a database has been set up on the PBX itself to store caller ID information, then `localhost` should be the value of the Host field.

 Housing a database with caller ID data on the same server that runs Asterisk can cause performance issues. On a server that routes a high volume of calls, the added load of performing a MySQL query against a local database will impact disk performance and reduce available processor resources. If MySQL will be used to store caller ID data, then it is best to host that caller ID database on a separate server from the PBX.

Database is the name of the database on the MySQL server.

Query is the SQL query string that will be used to retrieve names from the database. The query string must contain a placeholder for the telephone number that is being looked up. FreePBX will replace the special token [NUMBER] with the number to lookup. If the MySQL lookup was supposed to pull the value of a field called `cidname` from a table called `cidinfo`, then the query string might look like this: `SELECT cidname FROM cidinfo WHERE cidnumber LIKE '%[NUMBER]%'`.

The **Username** and **Password** fields are used to provide credentials that have access to the caller ID database. The user should be a MySQL user that has the ability to read the database. The user will not require permissions to insert new data or alter existing data in the database.

PIN Sets

A **Personal Identification Number (PIN)** is a numeric password that FreePBX can use to authenticate users when they attempt to dial specific features on the PBX such as outbound routes or DISA. Without entering a valid PIN, these features are inaccessible. A PIN set provides the ability for a group of PINs to be used to authenticate the use of a feature instead of just a single PIN. With a PIN set, each individual user can be given a unique PIN, and it is possible to revoke one user's access to a PBX feature without changing anyone else's PIN.

In addition to authenticating users, PIN sets can also be helpful in tracking which users used which features. When a PIN set is used as an authentication mechanism, FreePBX can log which unique PIN was used to access a feature in the `accountcode` column of the call detail records. Even if a user places a call from someone else's extension, they will need to enter their own account code. When generating a report of which users used certain features, the detail records will provide an accurate report based on which PINs were used. This feature is often used by companies which implement restrictions on long-distance calling. It is possible to track which users make heavy use of the long-distance outbound routes by checking the PINs used to dial out.

 As of FreePBX version 2.5.1, only outbound routes make use of the PIN sets feature. Future versions will expand the use of PIN sets to cover any PIN protected feature such as DISA and conferences.

In order to set up a PIN set, click on the **PIN Sets** link under the **Internal Options & Configuration** section of the navigation menu on the left side of the FreePBX interface as shown in the following screenshot:

PIN sets have only three configuration options:

1. **PIN Set Description**
2. **Record In CDR?**
3. **PIN List**

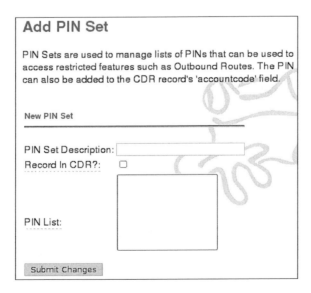

PIN Set Description is used to identify this PIN set when it is being selected during the configuration of an outbound route.

If the **Record In CDR?** checkbox is selected, then anytime a user authenticates themselves using this PIN set, the PIN they used will be stored in the `accountcode` field of the call detail records alongside the details of the call they made. This is a reliable method of tracking the usage of outbound routes, because even if a user calls from an extension other than their own, they still must enter their own PIN to place a call through a protected route. If this option is not enabled then the call is logged normally without any details in the `accountcode` field.

The **PIN List** is a list of one or more PIN codes. Each PIN should be on its own line. PINs can be as long as desired. However, as users are supposed to remember their PINs, it is typical to make PINs only four or five digits long.

A completed PIN set might look like the following:

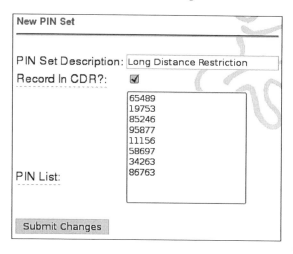

In order to put our new PIN set to use we must assign it to an outbound route. Click on the **Outbound Routes** link under the **Basic** section of the navigation menu on the left side of the FreePBX interface as shown in the following screenshot:

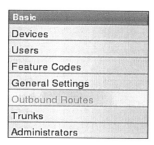

Click on the name of outbound route that the new PIN set will be associated with (in this example, **LongDistance**):

From the **PIN Set** drop-down menu, select the name of the new PIN set:

Click on the **Submit Changes** button at the bottom of the page followed by clicking on the orange-colored **Apply Configuration Changes** bar at the top of the page. All calls that pass through the selected outbound route will now be authenticated through one of the PINs in our new PIN set.

Misc applications

A misc application is a custom feature code. A misc application allows a custom extension or star code to be defined, which will direct the caller to any call target when dialed. For example, if we have a ring group that calls the cell phones of all staff members, we might create a misc application that calls that ring group when *CELL (*2355) is dialed.

In order to create a misc application, click on the **Misc Applications** link under the **Internal Options & Configuration** menu in the navigation menu on the left side of the FreePBX interface:

Misc applications have four configuration options:

1. **Description**
2. **Feature Code**
3. **Feature Status**
4. **Destination**

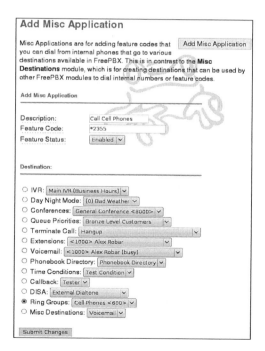

Description is used to identify this application if it needs to be edited or removed at a later time.

Feature Code is the custom feature code that users will dial in order to access this application. This can be a star code (for example, *1234) or simply a normal extension (for example, 1234). The value of this field must be unique (a misc application cannot share a feature code with any other user, application, or star code on the system).

Feature Status determines whether or not the application is active. If this field is set to **Disabled**, then users will be informed that the extension they dialed is not valid if they attempt to use the application. This field allows an application to be quickly disabled without having to remove the application entirely.

Destination is the call target that the application should route the caller to. Any call target that has been previously configured is a valid destination for a misc application.

Once all options have been configured, click on the **Submit Changes** button at the bottom of the page followed by the orange-colored **Apply Configuration Changes** bar at the top of the page. The application is now active and can be accessed by dialing the selected feature code from any extension on the PBX.

Misc Destinations

A misc destination is used to add a custom call target that can be used by FreePBX modules. Anything that can be dialed from a user's extension can be turned into a misc destination. For example, by default, there is no way to send an inbound caller directly to the messaging center so that the caller could log in and check their voicemail messages. A misc destination could be set up to dial *98 and then an inbound route could point directly to that misc destination. A caller who was routed through that inbound route would immediately hear the prompts to log into their voicemail box, just as if they were a user on the PBX and had dialed *98.

To create a misc destination, click on the **Misc Destinations** link under the **Internal Options & Configuration** menu in the navigation menu on the left side of the FreePBX interface as shown in the following screenshot:

Misc destinations have two configuration options and one quick pick drop-down field:

- **Description**
- **Dial**
- **--featurecode shortcuts--**

Description is used to identify this destination when it is being selected as a call target in other modules.

Dial is the extension, telephone number, or feature code that the system should dial when a caller is routed to this destination. Anything that can be dialed from a user's extension can be entered into this field.

The **--featurecode shortcuts--** drop-down menu lists all applications that are currently available on the PBX. Selecting an application from this menu will place a special token into the Dial field instead of an actual feature code or extension (for example, the token {voicemail:dialvoicemail} is placed in the field for the messaging center). This token acts as a dynamic link to the selected application. If the feature code for the chosen application changes, this destination will still continue to work. For example, the default feature code to access the voicemail messaging center is *98. If *98 is entered into the Dial field, the destination will work so long as the feature code to access the messaging center does not change. However, if at some point the feature code to access the messaging center is customized, this misc destination will still continue to dial *98, and anyone routed to the destination will receive a recording telling them that *98 is not a valid extension. Using a feature code shortcut avoids the risk of a destination breaking due to future customizations.

Once all options have been configured, click on the **Submit Changes** button at the bottom of the page followed by clicking on the orange-colored **Apply Configuration Changes** at the top of the page. The destination we just created will now be available as a call target from any other FreePBX module:

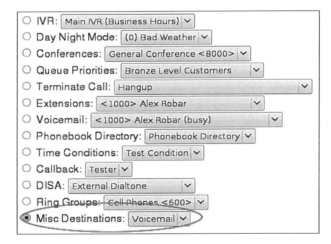

Summary

By now our PBX should truly be our own. In this chapter, we've learnt how to:

- Upload custom on-hold music
- Create on-hold music from streaming Internet sources
- Set up automated callback systems
- Configure DISA
- Configure custom caller ID lookup sources
- Configure PIN sets
- Create custom applications
- Create custom destinations

Our PBX is now entirely unique and customized to our specifications.

In the next chapter, we will discuss important topics such as system protection, backup and restoration, just in case disaster strikes.

10
System Protection, Backup and Restoration

After a lot of hard work and configuration, we finally have a fully-functional PBX configured precisely the way we need. Now, we need to make sure it stays that way. Even with the best hardware, the failure of a system component is a danger that is always present. Without proper protection and backups, we could wind up without a working PBX and have no way to restore it. In this chapter, we will discuss the following:

- System protection using UPS devices, redundant components, and surge protection
- Taking one-time backups
- Configuring recurring backups
- Restoring a backup
- Maintaining backup sets

System protection

There are many ways to protect the components of a server from failure or damage. While dealing with a PBX, these protection methods are even more important. As the PBX controls voice communications for a company, downtime often means lost income and angry employees.

While the installation and setup of the equipment listed here is beyond the scope of this book, it is worth keeping them in mind during installation.

Uninterruptible power supplies

An **Uninterruptible Power Supply (UPS)** is essential to every VoIP system. A UPS acts as a battery backup in the event of a power failure. If the power supply is cut, anything plugged into the UPS will continue to run until the battery runs out. Most UPS units will also be able to send a shutdown signal to the server when the battery is nearly empty, allowing a clean shutdown.

Some UPS units will also provide a power conditioning service, sending a stable level of power to any attached device. This protects any attached equipment from surges or dips on the power line that can be very damaging. Note that power conditioning is not included in all the makes and models of UPS, so be sure to check before purchasing.

Also note that for a VoIP PBX to continue to be truly effective during a power outage, it must be able to maintain an Internet connection for any VoIP trunk. It is generally a good idea to ensure that the UPS will power not only the PBX but also any modems, routers, and switches required for connectivity.

Redundant components

Most major server manufacturers provide the option for various types of redundant components. The most common redundant component is the hard drive, usually set up in a RAID configuration. This allows a hard drive to fail while the server keeps running. Power supplies are also a common redundant component, again allowing for one to fail without downing the server.

Though redundant components can be costly, they can often prevent downtime for the entire life of a PBX.

Redundant servers

Depending on the budget that is available for the PBX, it may be feasible to have an entirely separate server built and ready to take over call routing, in the event that the primary server fails. The secondary server may be running at all times and have a recent copy of all critical configuration data (known as running a **hot spare**). Alternately, it may be shutdown at all times, and only have a base installation of Linux, Asterisk, and FreePBX without any specific configuration data (known as running a **cold spare**).

A hot spare will usually be built using the same steps as the primary server. Once the primary server is configured with users, trunks, and call targets, the configuration data will need to be replicated from the primary server to the backup server. In less complicated setups, this can simply mean taking a backup on the primary server and restoring it on the hot spare. In order to ensure that data is current, the backup and restoration process should happen at least once per day. More complicated setups may have live replication of the MySQL database, Asterisk configuration files, the voicemail directories, so that when data is changed on the primary server the changes are reflected on the hot spare immediately.

Running a hot spare is typically an expensive endeavor. Initial hardware purchase cost is doubled, and as a hot spare is running at all times, the hardware components will tend to require replacements at the same time as the primary server's components. In addition, the manpower required to maintain data replication between the two servers is often very expensive. Nonetheless, if the budget exists for it, a hot spare will always be the most effective way to reduce downtime.

A cold spare will usually be built using the same steps as the primary server, until the point where the server is being configured with user accounts, trunks, and call targets. A cold spare will be left with a running FreePBX installation without any configuration on it. Regular backups of the primary server should be taken once it is fully configured. The cold spare will remain turned off during the normal operation of the primary server.

Whenever the system packages or FreePBX modules are updated on the primary server, the cold spare should be booted up to have the same updates applied to it. In the event that the primary server fails, the cold spare should be booted up and a recent FreePBX configuration backup should be restored to it. As with a hot spare, the initial hardware cost of running a cold spare is doubled. However, as a cold spare is rarely powered on, the hardware will tend to require replacement far less frequently than a hot spare, reducing the maintenance costs over time. Also, as data replication only happens in the event of a disaster, there is no additional cost for maintaining the data on the cold spare.

A cold spare is a good option if the implementation budget for the PBX allows for two sets of hardware, but maintenance does not allow for the expense of constantly replicating data.

Surge protection

The most common type of surge protection is for power lines, but surges can affect other components of the PBX that will impact functionality. If analog lines are in use with a ZAP card or ATA, a power surge down the phone lines can ruin equipment. A power surge down a cable or DSL line can take a modem out of operation, or any other routing equipment attached to it. It is important to install surge protection on these types of entry points to a PBX.

Backups

FreePBX allows a system backup of voicemails, system recordings, system configuration, CDRs, and Operator Panel configuration to be taken. Backups can be taken on a one-off basis, or a scheduled basis.

Backing up voicemail will back up all the voicemail messages and outgoing voicemail greetings for all the users configured on the system. If this is not backed up, then all the users will have to re-record their greetings, and they will be unable to retrieve historical voicemails which were received before the failure.

Backing up system recordings will back up all the voice prompts and custom music on hold recordings. Without this backup, prompts for IVRs, follow-me, queues, and music on hold recordings will all have to be re-recorded or reuploaded after a system failure.

Backing up system configuration will back up all the configuration data. This includes all of the configuration data for trunks, users, devices, IVRs, queues, time conditions — pretty much all the configuration data on the system. Without this backup, the system will have to be reconfigured all over again after a failure. This will be akin to starting from scratch.

Backing up CDR data will back up all the call detail records as far back as the system has them stored. Without this backup, if the system needs to be rebuilt all CDR records will be lost. There is no way to rebuild CDR records without this backup.

Backing up the Operator Panel will back up all the HTML and configuration data for the Flash Operator Panel. Without this backup, any FlashOP customizations will have to be completed again, and FlashOP will have to be reconfigured.

Taking a backup

In order to set up a backup, click on the **Tools** tab at the top of the navigation menu on the left:

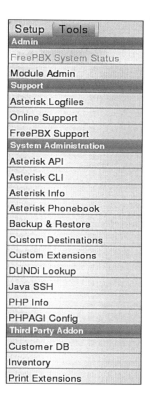

Click on **Backup & Restore**:

Click on **Add Backup Schedule** in the menu on the right:

The **System Backup** screen will be displayed as follows:

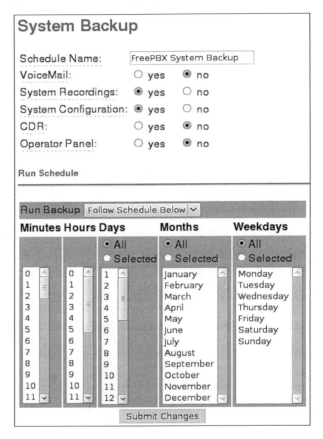

In the first section, select the items that should be backed up in this backup schedule. Note that a single FreePBX system can have multiple different backup schedules configured. It is possible to back up the **System Configuration** daily, **VoiceMail** weekly, and **System Recordings** and **CDR** monthly, if desired.

In order to fire off a one-time backup immediately, select **Now** from the **Run Backup** drop-down menu:

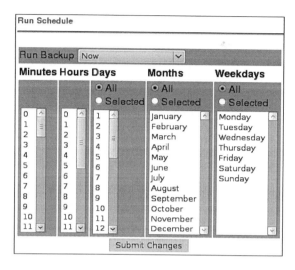

Setting up a one-time backup will immediately take a backup of the selected components as soon as the **Submit Changes** button is clicked on. The backup will occur only once.

In order to set up a scheduled backup instead of a one-time backup, select one of the predefined schedules from the **Run Backup** drop-down menu, or select **Follow Schedule Below** and select the appropriate schedule from the table. The schedule in the following screenshot will fire off the backup process at 6:30 a.m. on the 1st of every month:

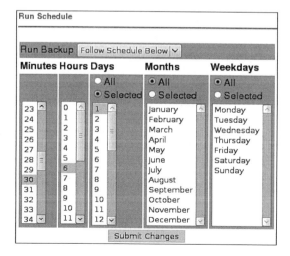

Click on the **Submit Changes** button in order to save the schedule. Once saved, the backup will show up in the menu on the right:

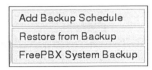

Clicking on the name of a schedule will load the **System Backup** screen, allowing the schedule and items that are being backed up to be edited.

Maintaining and protecting backups

The way in which FreePBX provides backups is simple and effective, but it presents two major problems: storage and protection. Similar to how call recordings have to be managed or they will fill up the available storage space, FreePBX backup schedules will continue to back up the system indefinitely. The backups must be maintained or the system will eventually run out of space and cease to function.

Once the problem of backup maintenance is taken care of, the problem of backup protection still exists. The backups taken by FreePBX reside on the server itself. If the hard disk crashes or the local backup becomes corrupted, there will be no way to restore a failed system.

Maintaining backups

Maintaining backups is best accomplished by a script that simply looks for backups older than a certain threshold and deletes them. The following script will search for all backups older than 90 days and delete them. The script can be adjusted to suit the appropriate backup retention policy for your PBX by changing the value of the BACKUPEXPIRY line as follows:

The following script is called OldBackupDeletion.sh:

```
#!/bin/bash

# Change this path to reflect your backup storage
# location (default is /var/lib/asterisk/backups)
BACKUPS=/var/lib/asterisk/backups

# Change this number to reflect the maximum age of
# backups (in days)
BACKUPEXPIRY=90
```

```
# Change this number to reflect the maximum age of the
# deletion logs (in days)
LOGEXPIRY=365
# Current date
DATE='date'

# Delete recordings older than $EXPIRY days
find $BACKUPS -mtime +$BACKUPEXPIRY -exec rm -rfv > removal-$DATE.log\

# Delete log files older than $LOGEXPRY
find . -mtime +$LOGEXPIRY -exec rm -rf\
```

This script can be run once daily to find backup sets older than the age limit and delete them. Adding the following line to cron will execute the script from /etc/backupdeletion daily at 5:00 a.m.:

```
0 5 * * * /etc/backupdeletion/OldBackupDeletion.sh
```

Protecting backups

There are a number of ways to protect backups. Each one may protect a particular deployment scenario better than the other. While the specifics of each protection scenario are outside the scope of this book, it is worth keeping them in mind when setting up backups to make sure that a backup is always close at hand. The most common methods for protecting backups are as follows:

- Redundant hardware (specifically, hard disks in a RAID configuration)
- Automating the copy of backups to an external hard disk or network location
- Automating the copy of backups to an off-site backup server or off-site backup service provider (using rsync, FTP, or similar scriptable methods)

Restoration

Backups taken by FreePBX can only be restored back to a running FreePBX system. In the event of a total failure, the operating system will have to be reinstalled along with FreePBX and MySQL, and backup archives will have to be copied back onto the server before a backup can be restored.

Restore to the same version of FreePBX only

Backups should always be restored to the same version of FreePBX that created the backup. A backup may be restored to a different version without error, but there is a good chance that something will be broken and cause further headaches down the line.

Every backup that is taken by FreePBX is stored in `/var/lib/asterisk/backups`. Each backup schedule has its own subfolder in this directory. If a backup is being restored to a newly built system, the original subfolder and all contained backup archives must first be copied to `/var/lib/asterisk/backups` before the backup will be accessible from within the FreePBX interface.

In order to start restoration of a backup, click on the **Tools** tab at the top of the navigation menu on the left:

Click on **Backup & Restore**:

Click on **Restore from Backup** in the menu on the right:

```
Add Backup Schedule
Restore from Backup
```

The **System Restore** screen will be displayed:

```
System Restore

• Weekly VM Backup
• Original System State Backup
• FreePBX System Backup
```

Every backup schedule that has been set up will be present in the restore menu (this includes both one-time backups and recurring backups). Click on the name of the backup set that is being restored to show a list of all available backup images from that backup schedule:

```
System Restore

• DELETE ALL THE DATA IN THIS SET

• 20090609.23.21.17.tar.gz
• 20090609.23.20.03.tar.gz
```

Images are titled by the date and time they were taken. Click on the name of the backup image that should be restored to show all data contained within the image:

```
System Restore

• Delete File Set

• Restore Entire Backup Set

• Restore VoiceMail Files

• Restore System Recordings Files

• Restore System Configuration

• Restore Operator Panel

• Restore Call Detail Report
```

The various links provide the ability to delete the set, restore the entire set, or selectively restore individual parts of a set. It is possible to restore multiple parts of a particular set individually.

In order to start restoration, click on the item that should be restored. FreePBX will warn about overwriting the item that is being restored.

> It is a good idea to take a full backup of all the FreePBX configuration data prior to attempting a restore. The restore process will completely overwrite all the existing configurations for the component that is being restored. If the wrong backup set is accidentally restored, then it is not possible to undo the changes.

Click on **OK** to proceed or **Cancel** to stop the restore:

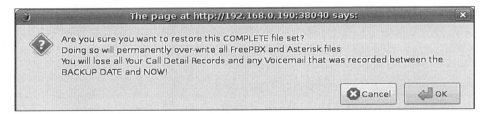

Once the restoration has completed be sure to click on the orange-colored **Apply Configuration Changes** bar at the top of the screen in order to reload all restored changes into the live configuration being used by Asterisk.

Summary

We are now prepared to handle disaster. We now know the appropriate steps that we should take in order to prevent the failure of our PBX. Our FreePBX system is backing itself up regularly, and we are maintaining and protecting those backups. In the unfortunate event of a systems failure, we are also prepared to restore from one of those backups.

In the next chapter, we will discuss the ins and outs of securing our PBX.

11
Security and Access Control

No matter which hardware platform it runs on, at the end of the day a FreePBX-based phone system is just like any other server. It runs on software that must be secured and maintained to ensure the system does not fall prey to hackers or malicious users. Given the nature of a PBX there is often no leeway afforded for downtime in the event that a system is compromised, so the best practice is to know how to protect the system to start with. In this chapter, we will discuss the following:

- Updating Linux operating system packages
- Maintaining a current version of Asterisk
- Securing the MySQL server
- Securing remote access to the PBX
- Securing FreePBX administration through administrator accounts

System packages

A FreePBX system runs on dozens of software packages that are constantly being updated. Updates to these packages fix bugs in their operation, and often patch security holes that could otherwise leave the system vulnerable to attacks. As with any upgrade, make sure that a backup exists just in case the updates cause something to break.

Depending on the distribution that is used and the amount of maintenance time afforded for upgrades, the frequency with which the system is updated can vary widely. In general, it is more than enough to update the system once per week. A standard schedule would update system packages once per month.

Different Linux distributions use different methods for updating packages. As the installation guide in this book discussed setting up Asterisk and FreePBX under Ubuntu and CentOS, commands for updating these distributions will be shown here. Be sure that you check how to update your system if you use a different distribution.

>
> **Safe packages**
>
> There is no "rule of thumb" as to which packages are safe and which are not. As the administrator of the PBX, you must be aware of critical package updates, including which are known to cause problems. It is a good idea to subscribe to the mailing lists for the distribution that you are running as a starting point for obtaining this information.

Updating Ubuntu Server

In order to update Ubuntu Server, first update the package list with the following command:

```
sudo apt-get update
```

Start the upgrade of all available packages:

```
sudo apt-get dist-upgrade
```

The system will provide a list of all the packages that are about to be installed. If the upgrades have dependencies that are not installed, the system will also list the new packages that need to be installed. Verify that the list contains safe upgrades, and then press the *Y* key followed by the *Enter* key in order to start the installation.

Once the updates are complete, the system will simply drop back to a shell. It is a good idea to go through the update process again until the system shows output similar to the following:

```
Building dependency tree
Reading state information... Done
Calculating upgrade... Done
0 upgraded, 0 newly installed, 0 to remove and 0 not upgraded.
```

Updating CentOS

In order to update CentOS, escalate to the root account at a shell and run the following command:

```
yum update
```

The system will update its list of available packages and then provide a summary of what is about to be performed:

```
Transaction Summary

==========================================

Install       4 Package(s)

Update       44 Package(s)

Remove        0 Package(s)

Total download size: 113 M

Is this ok [y/N]:
```

A list of packages that will be upgraded is listed above the **Transaction Summary**. Verify that the packages slated for upgrade are safe before pressing the *Y* key, followed by the *Enter* key in order to start the upgrade process.

Once the upgrade is complete, it is a good idea to go through the process again until the system reports that there is no new update to install.

Maintaining Asterisk versions

Just as the underlying system packages are updated, Digium releases updates to Asterisk whenever necessary in order to fix bugs or patch security concerns. If Asterisk was installed from source, it will not be updated when the system packages are updated. Updating Asterisk versions is very similar to the process of installing Asterisk.

Note that "updating" Asterisk in this context means to update Asterisk to a new release of the same major version that is currently running (for example, updating from 1.4.22 to 1.4.24). It does not mean updating between major release versions (for example, 1.4 to 1.6). Major version upgrades may be required during the life of a PBX, but these types of upgrades require special planning due to new features or features that may be deprecated or non-existent in the upgraded version (causing Asterisk to stop routing calls properly).

In order to make upgrades simple, Digium uses files that have the major version number suffixed with "-current" to denote the current version of Asterisk, Asterisk-Addons, Zaptel/DAHDI, and LibPRI. In the following examples, version 1.4 is being updated to the latest 1.4 release, but if the version on your PBX is different you can replace 1.4 with your major version release. In order to start upgrading Asterisk, we should first switch to the /usr/src directory:

```
cd /usr/src
```

Next, we need to make a backup of the previous tarballs that were used to install or update Asterisk. In case the upgrade to a new version encounters problems, it is always possible to move the older tarballs back into /usr/src and recompile them to reinstate the version of Asterisk that was running prior to the upgrade.

If this is the first time Asterisk is being upgraded, a backup folder will need to be created first (skip this step if the folder already exists from a previous upgrade):

```
mkdir asterisk-backup
```

Clear out the previous backups and then move the tarballs for the running version of Asterisk into the backup folder:

```
rm -rf asterisk-backup/*.tar.gz
mv asterisk-1.4*.tar.gz asterisk-backup/
mv asterisk-addons-1.4*.tar.gz asterisk-backup/
mv dahdi-linux-complete-*.tar.gz asterisk-backup/
mv libpri-1.4*.tar.gz asterisk-backup/
```

Next, remove the existing extracted source folders from previous updates (if they exist):

```
rm -rf asterisk-1.4*
rm -rf asterisk-addons-1.4*
rm -rf dahdi-linux-complete-*
rm -rf libpri-1.4*
```

Now download all current releases of the major versions of Asterisk, Asterisk-Addons, DAHDI, and LibPRI:

```
wget http://downloads.asterisk.org/pub/telephony/asterisk/asterisk-1.4-current.tar.gz
```

```
wget http://downloads.asterisk.org/pub/telephony/asterisk/asterisk-addons-1.4-current.tar.gz
```

```
wget http://downloads.asterisk.org/pub/telephony/dahdi-linux-complete/dahdi-linux-complete-current.tar.gz
```

```
wget http://downloads.asterisk.org/pub/telephony/libpri/libpri-1.4-current.tar.gz
```

Extract each of the tarballs:

```
tar zxf asterisk-1.4-current.tar.gz
tar zxf asterisk-addons-1.4-current.tar.gz
tar zxf dahdi-linux-complete-current.tar.gz
tar zxf libpri-1.4-current.tar.gz
```

Compile and install each of the downloaded packages:

```
cd libpri-1.4*
make; make install
cd ../dahdi-linux-complete-*
make; make install
cd ../asterisk-1.4*
./configure; make; make install
cd ../asterisk-addons-1.4*
./configure; make; make install
```

Finally, restart Asterisk:

```
amportal restart
```

If for any reason Asterisk fails to restart after an upgrade, be sure to check the Asterisk "full" log to see the source of the problem:

```
tail /var/log/asterisk/full
```

Securing MySQL

The MySQL database engine powers FreePBX. However, default settings on many distributions can easily make it one of the most vulnerable points on a server. Note that after the following suggestions are implemented, it is a good idea to restart the MySQL server (or just simply reboot the entire server) to force new settings to take effect.

MySQL passwords

The one biggest flaw that is often overlooked once a system is running is the passwords on the system's MySQL accounts.

If no passwords have been set on the accounts that were used to set up FreePBX, use the following code to set new passwords. The following examples assume that the FreePBX MySQL user is named "asterisk". If this is not the case with your PBX, you will need to adjust the sample command accordingly.

In order to set the root MySQL account password, use the following code:

```
mysqladmin -u root password NEWROOTPASSWORD
```

(Replace NEWROOTPASSWORD with the desired MySQL root password).

In order to set the asterisk MySQL account password, use the following code:

```
mysqladmin -u asterisk password NEWASTERISKPASSWORD
```

(Replace NEWASTERISKPASSWORD with the desired MySQL asterisk password).

Note that if the FreePBX MySQL user's password is changed, the new password must be updated in /etc/amportal.conf on the line that reads AMPDBPASS=.

Remove history

All MySQL commands that are run from the command line output their history to a file named .mysql_history in the user's home directory. This file stores all commands in clear text—including any passwords that were used. In order to clear this file, run the following command under each user account that ran MySQL commands:

```
cat /dev/null > ~/.mysql_history
```

Whenever the command line MySQL tools are used to administer MySQL user accounts, it is a good idea to run this command again to clear the history.

Disabling remote access to MySQL

As the web server that hosts the FreePBX interface is usually running on the same server that is running MySQL, remote access to the MySQL daemon can be disabled.

First, open /etc/mysql/my.cnf for editing:

```
nano /etc/mysql/my.cnf
```

Locate the [mysqld] section, and add the line bind-address = 127.0.0.1 to the bottom of the file. MySQL must be restarted for this configuration to take effect.

Remote access and lock down

The point at which a system is opened up so it can be remotely administered is almost always the point of compromise in an intrusion. It is a good idea to close off the system as much as possible from the outside world, in addition to locking down all network access to the server in general.

Changing ports

Changing the default ports that various services run on is a quick way to ward off the "script kiddie" style of hackers. This process essentially amounts to the "security through obscurity" model of protection. While it may not provide enough protection on its own, it provides a good first layer of protection.

In order to change the port that the SSD daemon listens on, run the following commands (this example changes the port to 38000; you can adjust this number according to your liking):

```
sed -i "s/Port 22/Port 38000/" /etc/ssh/sshd_config
/etc/init.d/ssh restart
```

In order to change the port that Apache listens on, run the following commands (this example changes the port to 38040; you can adjust this number according to your liking):

```
sed -i "s/Listen 80/Listen 38040/" /etc/apache2/ports.conf
/etc/init.d/apache2 restart
```

Changing VoIP ports

It is possible to change the ports that Asterisk listens on for SIP or IAX2 connections, but this is not recommended. VoIP endpoints connecting to the system will have to be specifically configured in order to change the ports they use, and sometimes this is not even supported. Changing the VoIP ports is almost always more trouble than it is worth.

Using iptables to restrict access

The iptables firewall is included with nearly all Linux distributions and provides one of the best forms of protection. Setting up the firewall to drop all traffic that isn't destined for services we are running improves the security of our PBX quite a bit. The iptables firewall is a complex software package, and proper configuration of the firewall is outside the scope of this book. However, if you choose to implement an iptables firewall, be sure to open the following ports:

- SSH (TCP port 22)
- Web/HTTP (TCP port 80)
- IAX2 (UDP port 4569)
- SIP Control (UDP port 5060)
- SIP RTP Stream (UDP ports 10000 through 20000)

Note that if any of the default service ports have been altered, then the appropriate ports will have to be opened in the iptables firewall.

It is also a good idea to restrict IP addresses that are able to access the SSH and web ports, if possible. If remote connections will come from a known set of IP addresses, then iptables can be set up to block SSH and HTTP requests if they do not originate from those IP addresses.

VPN or SSH tunnels

The most secure method of remote access is the one that does not exist directly at all. If the organization where the PBX will be deployed has an existing VPN solution, then the most secure way to access their FreePBX interface is over a VPN tunnel. In this case, iptables should be set up to only allow connections to administrative ports from the LAN IP range, and no administrative ports should be forwarded to the system at all from the edge router.

If no VPN exists, it is still possible to reduce the attack surface considerably by forcing web access to FreePBX through an SSH tunnel.

SSH tunneling under Linux

In order to generate an SSH tunnel under a Linux operating system, use a command similar to the following:

```
sudo ssh -L 80:<local ip>:80 <user>@<external ip>
```

<local ip> is the internal IP address of the server that is being connected to.

<user> is the username of the account that will be used to authenticate against the server being connected to.

<external ip> is the externally accessible IP address of the server being connected to.

For example, if a PBX has an internal IP of 1.1.1.1, an external IP of 2.2.2.2, and the user that we authenticate with is called "packtpub", our SSH command would look like the following:

```
sudo ssh -L 80:1.1.1.1:80 packtpub@2.2.2.2
```

The command maps port 80 locally to port 80 on the target machine. Once the SSH session is established, opening up a web browser and pointing it to `http://localhost:80` will load the FreePBX interface on the PBX.

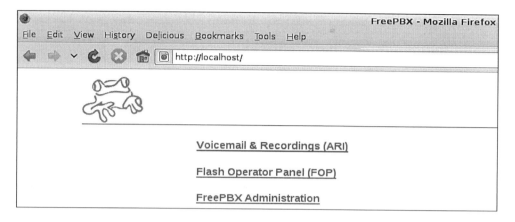

SSH tunneling under Windows

Generating SSH tunnels under Windows can be accomplished using a wonderful utility called PuTTY. PuTTY can be downloaded from `http://www.chiark.greenend.org.uk/~sgtatham/putty/`.

In order to set up an SSH tunnel in PuTTY, first enter the external IP address into the **Host Name (or IP address)** field:

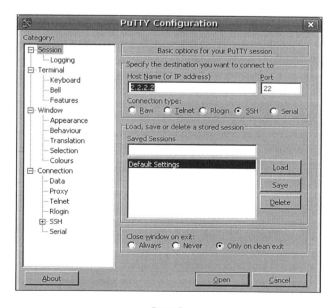

Expand **SSH** in the menu on the left (under **Connection**) and click on **Tunnels**:

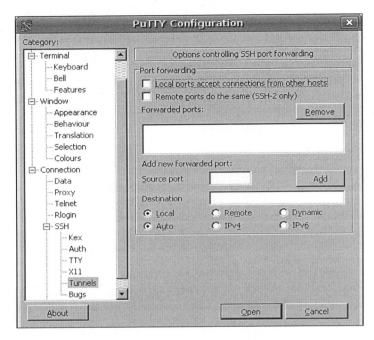

In the **Source port** field, type in 80.

In the **Destination** field, type in the internal IP address of the PBX server followed by a colon, and the port that Apache is running on (in this example, the server is at IP 1.1.1.1 and Apache runs on port 80 internally).

Leave all other settings at default and click on the **Add** button:

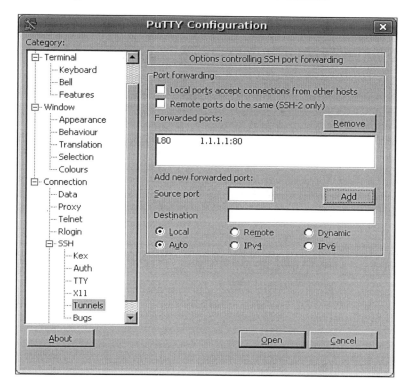

Click on the **Open** button to open the SSH tunnel. Once the tunnel is authenticated, FreePBX can be viewed by opening a web browser and browsing to `http://localhost:80`:

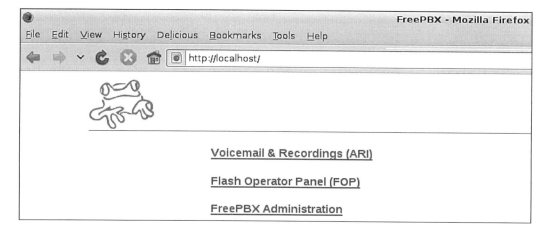

Administrator accounts in FreePBX

FreePBX incorporates the concept of different levels of administrator access. Administrator accounts can have their access restricted to specific departments, a specific extension range, or a specific set of modules. Separate administrator accounts should always be given out to anyone who administers the FreePBX system. Any staffing changes will then simply require a person's account to be removed to ensure they no longer have access.

Enabling administrator account authentication

By default, the Administrators module is not enabled. In order to check if the module is enabled, click on **Administrators** under **Basic** in the navigation menu on the left:

If the module is currently disabled there will be an error message displayed on the main page as shown in the following screenshot:

> General Settings
>
> **NOTE:**AUTHTYPE is not set to 'database' in /etc/amportal.conf - note that this module is not currently providing access control, and changing passwords here or adding users will have no effect unless AUTHTYPE is set to 'database'.

In order to correct this problem, log in to the PBX (either at the console or using SSH) and run the following two commands:

```
sudo sed -i "s/AUTHTYPE=none/AUTHTYPE=database/" /etc/amportal.conf
sudo /usr/src/AMP/apply_conf.sh
```

Once these commands have been run, FreePBX will prompt for a login whenever it is loaded. Before any administrator accounts have been created, the FreePBX database username and password will be the only functional login. This credential set would have been set up during the installation of FreePBX. If you are unsure what this login is, check the contents of /etc/amportal.conf. The lines that read AMPDBUSER= and AMPDBPASS= are the required username and password.

Managing administrator accounts and permissions

Once the Administrator module has been enabled, log in to FreePBX and click on **Administrators** under **Basic** in the navigation menu on the left:

The **Add Administrator** screen is shown:

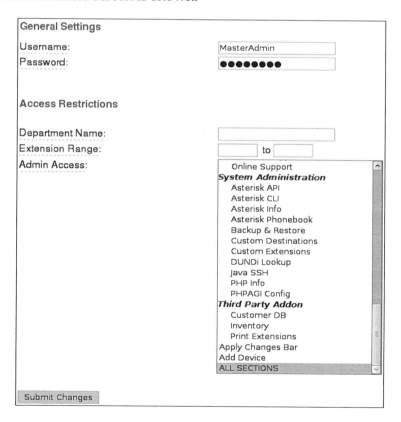

In the **Username** field, enter the account name for the user that is being set up. This is what the user will enter when prompted for username and password.

In the **Password** field, assign a password to the new user. Note that certain characters (such as an exclamation mark) have been known to cause problems in this field. It is best to stick with mixed case letters and numbers. Note that it is possible to create an administrator account that does not have a password. This is a dangerous practice and should be avoided.

The **Department Name** field is a great idea, but at the time of writing is not functional. This field is supposed to allow the user to be assigned to a specific department. When the Administrator module is enabled, certain call targets (such as IVRs and System Recordings) will have an additional field that will allow them to be owned by a specific department. Setting the Department Name field for an administrator will grant them access to all call targets that are in the same department without granting access to any other call targets in the same module. For example, if there is an IVR in the Sales department, an administrator with their Department Name set to sales will be able to change the settings on the Sales IVR but none of the other IVRs. Leaving this field blank will grant the administrator access to the call targets of all departments. Unfortunately, only the groundwork for this exists, the rest is not implemented. Setting this field will have no effect currently.

The **Extension Range** fields allow the administrator to be restricted to altering settings for a specific range of extensions. This is useful if extensions are specific to a department (for example, if the Sales department was extensions 250 through 299, granting a Sales administrator access to alter only these extensions may be useful). Leaving these fields blank allows the administrator to access all extensions.

The **Admin Access** field allows the administrator to be restricted to specific modules. In order to select multiple rows in Windows or Linux, *Ctrl + Click* on each desired row and on Mac, *Command/Apple + Click*. Each module that the administrator should have access to should be selected in this field. Note that **Apply Changes Bar** is a separate access module, so it is possible to give an administrator access to change something without giving them access to actually apply those changes.

Once all fields have been filled out appropriately click on the **Submit Changes** button followed by the orange-colored **Apply Configuration Changes** bar in order to make the new administrator active.

The administrator will show up in the menu on the right, and can be edited by clicking on their username:

Summary

By now we should be masters of the FreePBX realm. Our PBX should rival any of the competing closed-source solutions in terms of reliability, feature set, and security. Our system should now be locked down, allowing minimal access from outside the network. Each administrator should have their own login, and should be restricted to just the modules that they need to change.

A
FreePBX Modules

FreePBX has more than 50 optional modules available for installation from the online repository. A listing of all of the available modules and their functions as of the time of writing is as follows:

Basic

Module	Function
Built-in/Core	Provides basic call routing functionality and it is a built-in module. This includes Inbound Routes, Outbound Routes, Devices, Users, Extensions, and General Settings. The built-in module cannot be removed, and is installed by default when FreePBX is first installed.
Feature Code Admin	Provides the ability to enable/disable feature codes, or change the numbers that are dialed to access certain feature codes. Feature codes are extensions dialed by users to access certain PBX features such as call forwarding activation, voicemail, and call waiting activation.
FreePBX ARI Framework	Provides a way for updates to be installed for the Asterisk Recording Interface (a web interface for managing voicemails) through the FreePBX GUI.
FreePBX FOP Framework	Provides a way for updates to be installed for the Flash Operator Panel (a web interface for managing active calls) through the FreePBX GUI.
FreePBX Framework	Core framework for FreePBX. This is the framework that all of the other modules plug into. The framework encompasses the module administration page and the CDR/reporting pages.
FreePBX Localization Updates	Provides the ability to install translations of the FreePBX interface in localized languages.

Module	Function
System Dashboard	Provides a landing page that is shown whenever FreePBX is first logged into. The landing page shows the following pieces of information: • FreePBX Notices ° Notices when new modules are available for update ° Warnings when routes point to non-existent call targets ° Warnings when trunks or extensions have weak passwords ° Warnings when default MySQL or FreePBX passwords are in use ° Errors encountered by cron that are relevant to FreePBX (such as when a statistics gathering task fails) • FreePBX Statistics ° Total active calls ° Active internal calls (extension to extension) ° External calls (calls that are using an external trunk) ° Total active channels (how many people are actually speaking on the phone) ° IP phones online ° IP trunks online ° IP trunk registrations • Uptime ° System (operating system) uptime ° Asterisk uptime ° Last time Asterisk was reloaded • System Statistics ° Processor load average ° Processor current percent usage ° Physical memory in use ° Swap space in use ° Usage of all of the disk mount points ° Current send and receive statistics for all of the network interfaces
Voicemail	Provides the ability to configure voicemail for a user or extension. Voicemail cannot be used without this module.

CID and number management

Module	Function
Phonebook Directory	Provides an audio phonebook that users can search through from their telephones. The phonebook is populated from the FreePBX web interface. Users can search by name and are given the associated phone number when their search matches an entry.
Speed Dial Functions	Works in conjunction with the Phonebook Directory module. Entries in the phonebook can be assigned short speed dial codes that users can dial. Asterisk will then dial the associated full number of the phonebook entry and connect the call with the dialing user.

Games

Module	Function
Zork	An audio version of the text-based adventure game Zork. This module allows users to play Zork from their telephone handsets. The module uses a text-to-speech engine to read back the text generated by the Zork game engine.

Inbound call control

Module	Function
Announcements	Plays back a selected audio recording and then routes the call to another call target.
Blacklist	Provides the ability to build a list of numbers that are not allowed to call the system. Callers that are listed in the blacklist will hear a prompt informing them that the number they called is not in service.
Caller ID Lookup	Provides the ability to define various sources for caller ID names to be looked up against. Sources can be one of the following: • Internal (uses the Phonebook module to lookup names) • ENUM (uses ENUM DNS zones) • HTTP (uses an HTTP GET request against a hosted caller ID service) • MySQL (queries a MySQL database) Calls that are routed through the lookup module will try to match their calling number against the defined source. If a name is found, it will be displayed on the telephone handset that receives the call.

Module	Function
Day Night Mode	Provides the ability to configure a call target toggle. Two targets are defined and they can be toggled by a user, dialing a predefined extension. Calls routed through the module go to one of the destinations depending on the state of the toggle.
Follow Me	Provides the ability to create a personalized ring group for each user on the system. A set of phone numbers is configured to ring when the user's extension is rung, and a fail over destination is specified.
IVR	Provides digital receptionist functionality. The IVR module answers a call, plays back a sound clip, and waits for the caller to push digits on their phone in order to route the call.
Queue Priorities	Provides the ability to give a particular caller higher priority when entering a queue. Callers with higher priority will be placed at the front of the queue and have their calls answered faster.
Queues	Allows callers to be routed in a call queue where they wait on hold until someone is available to answer their call. Callers are placed into the queue in the order they called in (unless their call order is altered by a queue priority).
Ring Groups	Creates a call target that will ring a predefined set of extensions. Extensions can either be rung all at the same time or in various hunt sequences that ring one extension at a time.
Time Conditions	Provides the ability to route calls to one of two call targets depending on the day of the week, month, date, or time.

Internal options and configuration

Module	Function
Call Forward	Allows users to set up call forwarding from their extension to another extension by dialing a feature code.
Call Waiting	Allows users to toggle call waiting by dialing a feature code. When enabled, the user's phone will give an audio or visual indication that another call is coming in, if the user is already on the phone.
Callback	Allows a trigger to be configured that calls back a specific number and provides the callee with access to a module or application. The callback number can be predefined, or can be the number that triggered the callback. This is mostly used to provide a user's cell phone with a dial tone on the Asterisk system, giving them access to long distance calling that is cheaper than dialing directly from their cell phone.

Module	Function
Conferences	Provides the ability to set up conference rooms in which two or more users can join together in a single call. Conference rooms can be password protected.
DISA	Provides **Direct Inward System Access (DISA)** as a call target. This will give the caller a dial tone on the system allowing them to dial any of the features of the system, or initiate an outbound call through the trunks of the system.
Dictation	Allows a user to dial an extension, speak, and then have a recording of what they just said emailed to them.
Do-Not-Disturb (DND)	Allows a user to enable **Do-Not-Disturb (DND)** mode on their extension. If DND is enabled, calls to that extension will go straight to voicemail and the extension will not ring.
Info Services	Allows access to several information services through feature code for users. These services include: • Company directory • Call trace • Echo test • Speaking clock • Name current extension
Languages	Allows a call to be tagged with a specific language. The call can then be routed to a specific person or a set of people who speak the same language as the caller.
Misc Applications	Allows an administrator to configure arbitrary feature codes that direct the caller to a specific call target.
Misc Destinations	Allows an administrator to configure call targets that dial any local number (such as an extension, feature code, or external phone number). These destinations can then be set up as the target for inbound routes or as the failover destination for other call targets.
Music on Hold	Provides the ability to upload custom sound files or define streaming audio sources that will be played to callers while they are on hold.
PIN Sets	Allows an administrator to define a set of identification codes that can be used to grant access to outbound routes or conferences.
Paging and Intercom	Allows an administrator to define paging groups. When a paging group is called the phones in the group will automatically answer the call and play the caller's audio through their speakers. It also allows the creation of an intercom feature code that allows paging functionality to be directed to one phone specifically.

Module	Function
Parking Lot	Allows a call to be "parked". When a call is parked, the person parking the call is given a parking space number. Anyone who dials that number will be connected with the parked caller.
Recordings	Allows users to record, upload, and merge audio recordings. Recordings can be used in IVRs and as confirmation clips for ring groups.
Voicemail Blasting	Allows an administrator to create a group of extensions that can be "blasted" with a single voicemail message. When this functionality is invoked the caller records a message that is dropped into the voicemail box of all of the extensions that are members of the blast group.

Support

Module	Function
Asterisk Logfiles	Allows an administrator to view the Asterisk log files through the FreePBX web interface.
Online Support	Opens an **Internet Relay Chat (IRC)** session to the FreePBX IRC channel. FreePBX users and developers chat in this channel, and can provide support when asked.

System administration

Module	Function
Asterisk API	Provides the ability to create and edit users that can access the **Asterisk Manager Interface (AMI)**.
Asterisk CLI	Allows commands to be executed on the Asterisk Command Line Interface (Asterisk CLI) from the FreePBX web interface. CLI output is displayed in the web interface.

Module	Function
Asterisk Info	Provides the following information from Asterisk:

- Summary
  - ° Active SIP and IAX2 channels
  - ° Number of SIP and IAX2 registrations
  - ° Number of online and offline SIP and IAX2 peers

- Registries
  - ° Active SIP and IAX2 registrations (including registration host, username, refresh interval, and registration state)

- Channels
  - ° Active channel summary
  - ° Active number of SIP and IAX2 channels

- Peers
  - ° Shows all of the defined SIP and IAX2 extensions/peers

- SIP Info
  - ° Specific SIP registry and peer information

- IAX Info
  - ° Specific IAX2 registry and peer information

- Conferences
  - ° Shows details on conferences that are currently active

- Subscriptions
  - ° Shows registered dialplan hints

- Voicemail users
  - ° Shows a list of users that have a voicemail box and the number of waiting messages for those users

- Full report
  - ° Shows a full listing of all of the information contained within the other information sections

Module	Function
Backup & Restore	Provides the administrator with the ability to set up one-time or recurring backups of all of the FreePBX configuration data, recordings, and voicemails, and the ability to restore those backups.
Custom Applications	Allows customer applications and extensions to be registered with FreePBX so that they can be accessed by other FreePBX applications. These applications would be written into the extensions_custom.conf file.
DUNDi Lookup Registry	Allows an administrator to perform lookups against a Distributed Universal Number Discovery (DUNDi) cloud. The system must first be peered with another system using the DUNDi protocol for lookups to return any results.
Java SSH	Opens an embedded Java-based SSH client that connects to the host server.
PHP Info	Returns the output of the PHP function phpinfo(). This data includes the current PHP configuration, Apache configuration, active sessions, and environment variables.
PHPAGI Config	Allows an administrator to configure the PHP Asterisk Gateway Interface (AGI) application from the FreePBX web interface.
Phonebook Directory	Provides a phonebook that can be used as a lookup source for the Caller ID Lookup module. The phonebook is populated through the FreePBX web interface.
Weak Password Detection	Shows an administrator any user accounts, extensions, or trunks that have weak registration passwords. Accounts with weak passwords represent a security hole and should be updated as soon as possible.

Third-party add-on

Module	Function
Customer DB	If multiple companies are hosted on a single FreePBX system, the Customer DB module provides a way to track which company owns a particular trunk or SIP device. This module is simply for tracking purposes and does not affect configuration or call routing.
Gabcast	Provides integration with a third-party podcasting service— Gabcast. The Gabcast module adds the Gabcast service as an available call target for inbound routes or fail over destinations.
Inventory	Provides an inventory of all of the employees within a given company. The Inventory module provides places to enter the MAC address, IP address, and serial number of an employee's IP phone. This module is simply for tracking purposes and does not affect configuration or call routing.
Print Extensions	Provides a printable list of all of the configured extensions, conferences, queues, and feature codes.

B

Feature Codes

With all modules installed, FreePBX has more than 45 feature codes that users can dial to toggle features or run applications. Feature codes can be customized from the **Feature Code Admin** page (they can be located by clicking on the **Feature Codes** option under the **Basic** menu in the FreePBX interface). The default feature codes and their actions are listed as follows:

Blacklist

Feature code	Default	Action
Blacklist a number	*30	Prompts the user to enter a telephone number. The entered number is then added to the user's blacklist. Inbound calls will not ring an extension if they are on that extension's blacklist. Blacklisted callers will be told that the number they dialed is no longer in service.
Blacklist the last caller	*32	Adds the last number that called the user to the blacklist.
Remove a number from the blacklist	*31	Prompts the user to enter a telephone number. The entered number is removed from the user's blacklist.

Call Forward

Feature code	Default	Action
Call Forward All Activate	*72	Prompts the user to enter a phone number or extension number. Any calls to the user's extension will be forwarded to the entered number until call forwarding is deactivated.
Call Forward All Deactivate	*73	Deactivates call forwarding on the extension of the user placing the call.
Call Forward All Prompting Deactivate	*74	Prompts the user to enter an extension number. Call forwarding will then be disabled on the entered extension. This feature code enables a user to remove call forwarding on their extension from another extension on the system, or from any phone if the users have DISA access.
Call Forward Busy Activate	*90	Prompts the user to enter a phone number or extension number. If the user is on the phone from that point onward, inbound calls will be forwarded to the entered number. If the user is not on the phone when an inbound call comes in, the user's extension will ring as normal.
Call Forward Busy Deactivate	*91	Disables call forward on busy service, on the extension of the user placing the call.
Call Forward Busy Prompting Deactivate	*92	Prompts the user to enter an extension number. Call forward on busy service will then be disabled on the entered extension. This feature code enables a user to remove call forward on busy service from their extension using another extension on the system, or from any phone if the users have DISA access.
Call Forward No Answer/Unavailable Activate	*52	Prompts the user to enter a telephone number or extension number. If the user does not answer an inbound call or the user's telephone is not registered with Asterisk, inbound calls to the user will be forwarded to the entered number. If the user is on the phone when an inbound call comes in, the call will be processed normally (either by initiating call waiting or by failing over to another destination).
Call Forward No Answer/Unavailable Deactivate	*53	Disables call forward on no answer or unavailable service on the extension of the user placing the call.

Call Waiting

Feature code	Default	Action
Call Waiting Activate	*70	Enables call waiting service on the extension of the user placing the call. If an inbound call comes into an extension that is already on the line and call waiting is enabled, then the user receiving the call will hear a beep and may see the caller ID of the new caller (depending on their telephone). The user receiving the call can then place their current call on hold and pick up the new caller. Without call waiting, the new caller would either receive a busy signal or would immediately be dropped to voicemail without the extension ringing.
Call Waiting Deactivate	*71	Deactivates call waiting on the extension of the user placing the call.

Core

Feature code	Default	Action
Asterisk General Call Pickup	*8	Allows the user to pick up a call that is ringing another phone as long as the user's pickup group matches the ringing extension's call group. For example, if extension 5000 is in call group 1 and extension 5001 is in pickup group 1, the user at extension 5001 can pick up a call that is ringing extension 5000 by dialing *8. If the user's pickup group does not match the call group of the ringing phone, dialing this feature code will have no effect.
ChanSpy	555	Allows the user to listen to an active call. After initiating the ChanSpy application, the user can dial the * key to cycle through all active channels.
Dial System FAX	666	Dials the extension that is defined as the default fax extension. The default fax extension is set on the General Settings page by changing the extension of the fax machine for the receiving faxes drop-down menu.
Directed Call Pickup	**(ext)	Allows the user to pick up a call directed to another extension. The (ext) token should be replaced with the extension being picked up. For example, if extension 5001 is ringing, another user could dial **5001 to pick up the call.

Feature code	Default	Action
In-Call Asterisk Attended Transfer	*2	When on a call, a user can dial this feature code to initiate an attended transfer. The user will hear a dial tone and at this point, they can enter an extension or telephone number. The users will be connected with the number they dialed. When the user hangs up the phone, the person they are transferring will be connected with the person the user called. Attended transfers are used when the person transferring the call wishes to speak to the person receiving the call before the call is transferred. A common scenario for this would be a call center agent transferring a call to their manager. The agent needs to first brief the manager on the problem before the call is transferred.
In-Call Asterisk Blind Transfer	##	When on a call, a user can dial this feature code to initiate a blind transfer. The user will hear a dial tone and at this point, they can enter an extension or telephone number. The person the user was speaking with will be immediately transferred to the number the user entered.
In-Call Asterisk Disconnect Code	**	When on a call, a user can dial this feature code to immediately terminate the call.
In-Call Asterisk Toggle Call Recording	*1	When on a call, a user can dial this feature code to start the recording of the call using the Asterisk MixMonitor application. This feature code works if the user's **Recording Options** are set to **On Demand** on their configuration page in the FreePBX interface. Recorded calls are saved to the /var/spool/asterisk/monitor directory by default.
Simulate Incoming Call	7777	Simulates an inbound call to the PBX. The call will be matched against any inbound route rules in the same way as an incoming call through a trunk would be matched.
User Logon	*11	If FreePBX is configured in the DeviceAndUser mode, this feature code will allow a user to log in to a telephone with their extension and password. Once a user is logged in, any calls to the user's extension will ring the phone the user logged into.

Feature code	Default	Action
User Logoff	*12	If FreePBX is configured in DeviceAndUser mode, this feature code will allow a user to log out of a phone they are currently logged into. If a user is not logged in to any device when a call comes into their extension, the call will immediately proceed to the user's failover destination (this is normally voicemail, but it can be other extensions or telephone numbers if follow-me is configured).
ZapBarge	888	Prompts the user for a channel number. The user will then be able to listen to an active call on the Zap or DAHDI channel, which they entered. ZapBarge has been renamed to DAHDIBarge in newer releases due to trademark violations.

Day Night Mode

Feature code	Default	Action
Toggle Day Night Mode	*28(num)	The token (num) should be replaced with a single-digit number between 0 and 9 that corresponds to the index of the Day Night Mode being toggled. Dialing this feature code will toggle the state of the Day Night Mode index that was selected. For example, to toggle the Day Night Mode with index 3, dial *283.

Dictation

Feature code	Default	Action
Perform dictation	*34	Prompts the user to enter a numeric filename followed by the pound (#) key. The user is then connected to the dictation application where whatever they say will be recorded. The dictation application allows recording to be paused at will, and can be switched to playback mode to hear the current recording.
Email completed dictation	*35	Prompts the user to enter a numeric filename followed by the pound (#) key. If a dictation recording with that filename exists, it will be emailed to the email address specified in the user's dictation options in the FreePBX interface.

Do-Not-Disturb (DND)

Feature code	Default	Action
DND Activate	*78	Activates the Do-Not-Disturb (DND) mode for the extension placing the call. Any calls directed to an extension with DND enabled will not ring any of the phones associated with that extension. Calls to an extension that has DND enabled will immediately continue to the extension's failover destination (this is usually voicemail, but could be other extensions or phone numbers if follow me is enabled).
DND Deactivate	*79	Deactivates the Do-Not-Disturb (DND) mode for the extension placing the call.
DND Toggle	*76	Toggles the state of Do-Not-Disturb (DND) mode for the extension placing the call.

Follow Me

Feature code	Default	Action
Findme Follow Toggle	*21	Toggles follow-me mode on the extension placing the call. Any calls to an extension with follow me enabled will follow the call flow defined in the extension's Follow Me configuration page in the FreePBX interface. If follow me is disabled, calls to the extension will ring any associated phones as normal, and fail over to voicemail (if enabled) or eventually disconnect the call (if voicemail is not enabled).

Info Services

Feature code	Default	Action
Call Trace	*69	Plays back the telephone number or extension number of the last caller to the phone dialing the feature code.
Directory	#	Connects the user to the company directory. The directory is populated with all users who have voicemail boxes. The directory can be searched by first name and last name (this is a configurable option on the FreePBX General Settings page). When a user finds the person they are looking for, they can opt to be transferred to that person.

Feature code	Default	Action
Echo Test	*43	Plays back whatever the user is saying as they are saying it. The echo test is designed to provide a sense of the latency between the telephone dialing the feature code and the Asterisk server.
Speak Your Exten Number	*65	Plays back the extension number of the extension placing the call.
Speaking Clock	*60	Plays back the current time on the Asterisk server.

Paging and Intercom

Feature code	Default	Action
Intercom prefix	*80(ext)	Connects the user to another extension via intercom functionality (the called phone does not ring, but immediately answers the call and places the call on speaker phone). The (ext) token should be replaced with the extension that the user is trying to connect to. For example, to start an intercom session with extension 5001, dial *805001. The extension being called must have intercom functionality enabled, and the phone must support auto-answer via SIP info headers. Most SIP phones provide this support.
User Intercom Allow	*54	Enables intercom functionality on the extension placing the call. Any user can initiate an intercom session with an extension that has this functionality enabled.
User Intercom Disallow	*55	Disables intercom functionality on the extension placing the call. If intercom functionality is disabled on an extension, any user who tries to initiate an intercom session with that extension will hear a message indicating that all circuits are busy, and hence the session will not be established.

Phonebook Directory

Feature code	Default	Action
Phonebook dial-by-name directory	411	Works in conjunction with the FreePBX Asterisk Phonebook module. The user is prompted to enter three letters on their touch tone phone to make a search in the phonebook. When the desired entry is found, the user is given the option to press 1 to dial the phone number associated with the matching entry.

Recordings

Feature code	Default	Action
Save Recording	*77	Plays a single beep after which whatever the user says is recorded to a temporary file on the PBX. This is used in conjunction with the FreePBX System Recordings module. The FreePBX interface is used to name the temporary recording and transfer it to a more permanent location.
Check Recording	*99	Plays back the most recent temporary recording that was made by the user placing the call. It is used to verify that a recording sounds the way it was meant to. If the user is not satisfied with the recording, they can dial the Save Recording feature code again to re-record it.

Speed Dial Functions

Feature code	Default	Action
Set user speed dial	*75	Allows the user to configure a speed dial entry. The user is prompted for a speed dial location followed by the pound (#) key. The speed dial location can be any number. The user is then prompted for the telephone number or extension number, which they wish to add to speed dial followed by the pound (#) key. For example, to add the phone number 555-555-1234 to the speed dial location 1000, dial *75, wait for the prompt, then dial *1000#* and wait for the prompt, and now dial *5555551234#*.
Speeddial prefix	*0(num)	The (num) token should be replaced by the speed dial location being dialed. Dialing this feature code connects the user with the speed dial phone number associated with the speed dial location they entered. For example, to dial the telephone associated with speed dial location 1000, dial *01000*.

Voicemail

Feature code	Default	Action
Dial Voicemail	*98	Prompts the user to enter a voicemail box number and the password associated with that mailbox. If the user is authenticated successfully, they are transferred to the messaging center where they can listen to their voicemails and record their outgoing voicemail messages.
My Voicemail	*97	Assumes the user is calling to check messages in the voicemail box associated with the extension they are calling from. It prompts the user for a password. If the user is authenticated successfully, they are transferred to the messaging center where they can listen to their voicemails and record their outgoing voicemail messages.

C

Voicemail.conf Options

When setting up an extension (Extensions mode) or a user (DeviceAndUser mode), FreePBX provides a field called **VM Options** under the **Voicemail & Directory** group of options. This field allows any option to be entered that could be included as a mailbox option in /etc/asterisk/voicemail.conf. These options affect the behavior of a mailbox and the way the voicemail messages are received and processed.

Options should be listed using the syntax optionname=value (where optionname is replaced with the name of the option being configured, and value is replaced with a valid value for that option). Multiple options can be specified by placing a pipe character (|) between each option (for example, attach=yes|attachfmt=gsm).

Option	Valid values	Purpose
attach	yes, no	If voicemail to email notifications are enabled, the attach option allows a copy of the voicemail to be attached to the email notification. If this option is not configured, the default value of "no" will be used by Asterisk. Note that this option can be configured within the FreePBX interface using the **Email Attachment** field and should not be manually configured. Manually configuring this option could result in conflicting configurations and unpredictable results.

Option	Valid values	Purpose
attachfmt	gsm, wav, wav49	Specifies the format that the sound file attached to the notification email should be in. GSM files are raw GSM encoded, WAV files are 16-bit linear WAV encoded, and WAV49 files are GSM encoded WAV format files. Windows PCs can play back WAV files by default, and most stock Linux desktop PCs should be able to play back GSM files. Any operating system should be able to play any of these formats, but additional software may be required. If this option is not configured, the default value of "wav" will be used by Asterisk.
callback	(Any valid context)	The Asterisk voicemail applications provide the ability for a user to call back the telephone number or extension number of the person who left them a voicemail. The callback option configures the context that Asterisk will use for placing the outbound call. By default, users created under FreePBX use the from-internal context to place their calls, and this option can be safely set to this value.
		The only time this option typically differs from the context that the user normally utilizes is when a user's outbound calling ability is restricted. If a user can typically call local telephone numbers, but not long distance, they would be unable to return a voicemail from anyone who is not within the local calling area. It is prudent for a company to allow callbacks to someone who has left a message. A company may choose to create a special context specifically for the purpose of voicemail callbacks in which calls to long distance numbers are allowed. In this case, the callback option would be set to the name of the custom context that allows long distance calling.
		If this option is not configured, no default value will be used and the callback feature of the voicemail application will be disabled.

Option	Valid values	Purpose
delete	yes, no	If voicemail to email notifications are enabled, the `delete` option provides the ability to delete voicemail messages from the Asterisk server as soon as the notification email is sent. This option is intended to be used by users who wish to receive their voicemails through email *only*. If this option is not configured, the default value of "no" will be used by Asterisk. Note that this option can be configured within the FreePBX interface using the **Delete Voicemail** field and should not be manually configured. Manually configuring this option could result in conflicting configurations and unpredictable results.
envelope	yes, no	If set to "yes", the user will hear the date and time a message was left prior to the message being played when they check their messages.
forcegreetings	yes, no	If set to "yes", new users will be prompted to record their busy and unavailable outgoing messages the first time they log into their mailbox. The voicemail application determines that a user is new if their voicemail password is the same as their extension. If this option is not configured, the default value of "no" will be used by Asterisk.
forcename	yes, no	If set to "yes", new users will be prompted to record their name the first time they log into their mailbox. The voicemail application determines that a user is new if their voicemail password is the same as their extension. If this option is not configured, the default value of "no" will be used by Asterisk.
hidefromdir	yes, no	If set to "yes", the user will be hidden from the company directory. If this option is not configured, the default value of "no" will be used by Asterisk.

Option	Valid values	Purpose
imapuser/ imappassword	(IMAP account credentials)	The voicemail application allows voicemail messages to be stored on an IMAP server as of Asterisk version 1.4. Storing messages on an IMAP server allows voicemail to be managed either through a phone or an email client. Changes made using one management method are reflected in the other. For IMAP storage to work, the file /etc/asterisk/ vm_general.inc must be edited in order to include a line that reads imapserver=servername (where servername is replaced with the actual hostname of the IMAP server being used). Once the imapserver configuration option is defined in the vm_general.inc file, the imapuser and imappassword options must be configured to use valid user account credentials for the IMAP server. If these options are not configured, there are no default values used, and IMAP voicemail storage will not be used.
maxmsg	(whole number)	Defines the maximum number of messages that the user can have in each one of their voicemail folders. If this option is not configured, then there is no default value used and no limit will be placed on the amount of voicemail messages a user can store.
operator	yes, no	If set to "yes", the person leaving the message is able to press 0 to return to the call target they came from before dialing an extension. For example, if a caller is directed to an IVR and then dials a user's extension and receives voicemail, they can press 0 to return to the IVR. If the caller did not come from a previous call target (they were routed directly to the user's extension), pressing 0 will route their call to the extension defined in the **Operator Extension** field on the FreePBX **General Settings** page. If this option is not configured, the default value of "no" will be used by Asterisk.
review	yes, no	If set to "yes", the person leaving the message is able to press the pound (#) key after leaving their message in order to review the message they just recorded. They are given the option to re-record their message if they choose to. If this option is not configured, the default value of "no" will be used by Asterisk.

Option	Valid values	Purpose
saycid	yes, no	If set to "yes", the user will hear the caller ID number of the person who left the voicemail prior to the voicemail being played when they check their messages. If this option is not configured, the default value of "no" will be used by Asterisk. Note that this option can be configured within the FreePBX interface using the **Play CID** field and should not be manually configured. Manually configuring this option could result in conflicting configurations and unpredictable results.
sayduration	yes, no	If set to "yes", the user will hear the duration of the voicemail message prior to the voicemail being played when they check their messages. If this option is not configured, the default value of "no" will be used by Asterisk.
saydurationm	(Minimum time, in whole number of minutes)	This option restricts when the voicemail application will say the duration of a message. If this value is set, then the voicemail application will only announce the duration of a message if the message is longer than the value of `saydurationm`. For example, if this option is set to "2", the application will only announce the duration of messages that are longer than two minutes. This option only takes effect when the `sayduration` option is set to "yes". If this option is not configured, no default value will be used and all message durations will be announced when the `sayduration` option is set to "yes".
sendvoicemail	yes, no	If set to "yes", the user is able to forward a voicemail message they have received to another user. Otherwise, this functionality is disabled. If this option is not configured, the default value of "no" will be used by Asterisk.
serveremail	(Email address)	This option sets the email address from which voicemail to email notification messages appear to come. For example, this might be `voicemail@example.com`.
tempgreetwarn	yes, no	If set to "yes" and the user has a temporary greeting enabled, they will be notified that the greeting is enabled each time they check their voicemail messages. If this option is not configured, the default value of "no" will be used by Asterisk.

Option	Valid values	Purpose
tz	(Valid timezone)	This option specifies which time zone a user is in, so that the envelope time data is played in the user's local time instead of the server's local time. This option must be a valid time zone. In order to find the valid time zones on the FreePBX server, check the contents of the /usr/share/zoneinfo folder. The files in this folder are valid time zones; the subfolders contain country-specific time zones. If this option is not configured, the default time zone will be the local time zone of the FreePBX server.
volgain	(Positive or negative numbers, rounded to one decimal place)	Specifies the gain that should be used when recording messages for the user. If messages are generally too quiet, the value should be higher (for example, 1.5). If messages are too loud, the number should be lower (for example, -2.1). If this option is not configured, the default value of "0" will be used by Asterisk and no gain will be applied to voicemail messages.

D

Common Trunk Configurations

The trunk configuration settings for common VoIP providers are as follows. Simply replace the required information tokens in the following configurations with their appropriate values to configure a fully working trunk.

Required information tokens that may be used are listed as follows:

Token	Replace with
(Name)	The name of the owner of the trunk. This might be a company's name or a person's name. Letters, numbers, and spaces are allowed. No other special characters may be used.
(TelNumber)	The telephone number associated with the trunk that is being configured. For PSTN trunks, this will be a number in the format of the local calling area (for example, nine digits for North America). Trunks to other VoIP providers may have different formats. For example, the **Free World Dialup (FWD)** network uses six-digit telephone numbers.
(Username)	The username or user ID assigned by the VoIP provider. This is usually a numeric user ID.
(Password)	The password or "secret" assigned by the VoIP provider.
(MaxChannels)	The maximum number of active channels that the provider can support. Some providers have a set limit (in which case that limit will be listed). Some providers allow the purchase of additional channels for which a monthly fee is charged (in this case, the (MaxChannels) token is used).
(FailureScript)	The script that is used to monitor trunk failures, if one exists. See the *Monitoring trunk status with FreePBX failure scripts* section of Chapter 4, *Trunks* for sample monitoring scripts.
(VoIPHost)	The SIP or IAX2 server supplied by the provider. This might be referred to as the "registration server" or simply the "host" by the provider.

FreePBX SIP by Bandwidth.com

- Protocol: SIP
- Type: Monthly unlimited or per minute

Field	Value
Outbound Caller ID	(TelNumber)
Never Override CallerID	unchecked
Maximum Channels	(MaxChannels)
Disable Trunk	unchecked
Monitor Trunk Failures	(FailureScript)
Dial Rules	1+NXXNXXXXXX
Dial Rules Wizards	not applicable
Outbound Dial Prefix	
Trunk Name	freepbx
PEER Details	type=peer
	insecure=very
	host=(VoIPHost)
	quality=yes
	sendrpid=yes
	username=(Username)
	secret=(Password)
	context=from-pstn
USER Context	freepbx-in
USER Details	type=user
	context=from-pstn
	host=(VoIPHost)
Register String	(Username):(Password)@(VoIPHost)

Unlimitel (SIP)

- Protocol: SIP
- Type: Per minute

Field	Value
Outbound Caller ID	"(Name)" <(TelNumber)>
Never Override CallerID	unchecked
Maximum Channels	5
Disable Trunk	unchecked
Monitor Trunk Failures	(FailureScript)
Dial Rules	1+NXXNXXXXXX
Dial Rules Wizards	not applicable
Outbound Dial Prefix	
Trunk Name	(TelNumber)-out
PEER Details	disallow=all
	allow=ulaw
	canreinvite=no
	context=from-pstn
	dtmfmode=rfc2833
	host=(VoIPHost)
	username=(TelNumber)
	secret=(Password)
	insecure=port,invite
	progressinband=no
	relaxdtmf=yes
	rfc2833compensate=yes
	type=peer
USER Context	(TelNumber)-in

Field	Value
USER Details	disallow=all
	allow=ulaw
	canreinvite=no
	context=from-pstn
	dtmfmode=rfc2833
	host=sip.unlimitel.ca
	username=(TelNumber)
	secret=(Password)
	insecure=port,invite
	progressinband=no
	relaxdtmf=yes
	rfc2833compensate=yes
	type=peer
Register String	(TelNumber):(Password)@(VoIPHost)/ (TelNumber)

Unlimitel (IAX2)

- Protocol: IAX2
- Type: Per minute

Field	Value
Outbound Caller ID	"(Name)" <(TelNumber)>
Never Override CallerID	unchecked
Maximum Channels	5
Disable Trunk	unchecked
Monitor Trunk Failures	(FailureScript)
Dial Rules	1+NXXNXXXXXX
Dial Rules Wizards	
Outbound Dial Prefix	
Trunk Name	(TelNumber)

Field	Value
PEER Details	disallow=all
	allow=ulaw
	context=from-pstn
	host=(VoIPHost)
	secret=(Password)
	type=friend
	canreinvite=no
	username=(TelNumber)
USER Context	(TelNumber)-in
USER Details	disallow=all
	allow=ulaw
	canreinvite=no
	context=from-pstn
	type=friend
Register String	(TelNumber):(Password)@(VoIPHost)

SIPGate

- Protocol: SIP
- Type: Per minute

Field	Value
Outbound Caller ID	"(Name)" <(TelNumber)>
Never Override CallerID	unchecked
Maximum Channels	1
Disable Trunk	unchecked
Monitor Trunk Failures	(FailureScript)
Dial Rules	1+NXXNXXXXXX
Dial Rules Wizards	
Outbound Dial Prefix	
Trunk Name	SIPGate

Field	Value
PEER Details	disallow=all
	allow=ulaw&alaw
	context=from-pstn
	disallow=all
	fromdomain=sipgate.com
	fromuser=(Username)
	host=sipgate.com
	insecure=invite
	nat=no
	secret=(Password)
	type=peer
	username=(Username)
USER Context	
USER Details	
Register String	(TelNumber):(Password)@sipgate.com/ (TelNumber)

Teliax (SIP)

- Protocol: SIP
- Type: Per minute

Field	Value
Outbound Caller ID	"(Name)" <(TelNumber)>
Never Override CallerID	unchecked
Maximum Channels	(MaxChannels)
Disable Trunk	unchecked
Monitor Trunk Failures	(FailureScript)
Dial Rules	1+NXXNXXXXXX
Dial Rules Wizards	
Outbound Dial Prefix	
Trunk Name	Teliax

Field	Value
PEER Details	disallow=all
	allow=ulaw
	dtmfmode=inband
	canreinvite=no
	host=(VoIPHost)
	insecure=invite
	nat=yes
	qualify=yes
	secret=(Password)
	type=friend
	username=(Username)
USER Context	Teliax-in
USER Details	disallow=all
	allow=ulaw
	dtmfmode=inband
	canreinvite=no
	context=from-pstn
	insecure=invite
	type=user
Register String	(Username):(Password)@proxy.teliax.net

Teliax (IAX2)

- Protocol: IAX2
- Type: Per minute

Field	Value
Outbound Caller ID	"(Name)" <(TelNumber)>
Never Override CallerID	unchecked
Maximum Channels	(MaxChannels)
Disable Trunk	unchecked
Monitor Trunk Failures	(FailureScript)
Dial Rules	1+NXXNXXXXXX
Dial Rules Wizards	
Outbound Dial Prefix	
Trunk Name	Teliax
PEER Details	disallow=all
	allow=ulaw
	canreinvite=no
	host=(VoIPHost)
	insecure=invite
	nat=yes
	qualify=yes
	secret=(Password)
	type=friend
	username=(Username)
USER Context	Teliax-in
USER Details	type=user
	context=from-pstn
Register String	(Username):(Password)@proxy.teliax.net

BroadVoice

- Protocol: SIP
- Type: Monthly unlimited

Field	Value
Outbound Caller ID	"(Name)" <(TelNumber)>
Never Override CallerID	unchecked
Maximum Channels	(MaxChannels)
Disable Trunk	unchecked
Monitor Trunk Failures	(FailureScript)
Dial Rules	1+NXXNXXXXXX
Dial Rules Wizards	
Outbound Dial Prefix	
Trunk Name	Broadvoice
PEER Details	disallow=all
	allow=ulaw&alaw
	context=from-trunk
	dtmf=auto
	dtmfmode=inband
	fromdomain=sip.broadvoice.com
	fromuser=(TelNumber)
	host=sip.broadvoice.com
	insecure=port,invite
	qualify=yes
	secret=(Password)
	type=peer
	user=(TelNumber)
	username=(TelNumber)
USER Context	
USER Details	
Register String	(TelNumber):(Password)@sip.broadvoice.com/(TelNumber)

Gizmo5

- Protocol: SIP
- Type: Free (SIP to SIP) and per minute

Field	Value
Outbound Caller ID	"(Name)" <(TelNumber)>
Never Override CallerID	unchecked
Maximum Channels	(MaxChannels)
Disable Trunk	unchecked
Monitor Trunk Failures	(FailureScript)
Dial Rules	1747XXXXXXX
	1+747XXXXXXX
	010+1XXXXXXXXX
	0101+XXXXXXXXX
Dial Rules Wizards	
Outbound Dial Prefix	
Trunk Name	Gizmo5
PEER Details	disallow=all
	allow=ulaw&alaw&ilbc
	canreinvite=no
	context=from-trunk
	dtmfmode=rfc2833
	fromdomain=proxy01.sipphone.com
	fromuser=(TelNumbeR)
	host=proxy01.sipphone.com
	insecure=very
	secret=(Password)
	type=peer
	username=(TelNumber)
USER Context	
USER Details	
Register String	(TelNumber):(Password)@proxy01.sipphone.com

SIP Broker

- Protocol: SIP
- Type: Per minute

Field	Value
Outbound Caller ID	"(Name)" <(TelNumber)>
Never Override CallerID	unchecked
Maximum Channels	(MaxChannels)
Disable Trunk	unchecked
Monitor Trunk Failures	(FailureScript)
Dial Rules	1+NXXNXXXXXX
Dial Rules Wizards	
Outbound Dial Prefix	
Trunk Name	sipbroker-out
PEER Details	disallow=all
	allow=g729&ulaw&alaw
	canreinvite=no
	dtmfmode=rfc2833
	fromdomain=(Username)
	fromuser=(Username)
	host=sipbroker.com
	insecure=very
	nat=yes
	port=5060
	secret=(password)
	type=peer
USER Context	
USER Details	
Register String	

Via Talk

- Protocol: SIP
- Type: Yearly unlimited

Field	Value
Outbound Caller ID	"(Name)" <(TelNumber)>
Never Override CallerID	unchecked
Maximum Channels	(MaxChannels)
Disable Trunk	unchecked
Monitor Trunk Failures	(FailureScript)
Dial Rules	1+NXXNXXXXXX
Dial Rules Wizards	
Outbound Dial Prefix	
Trunk Name	viatalk
PEER Details	disallow=all
	allow=ulaw
	authuser=(TelNumber)
	context=from-trunk
	dtmf=auto
	dtmfmode=inband
	fromdomain=(VoIPHost)
	fromuser=(TelNumber)
	host=(VoIPHost)
	insecure=port,invite
	qualify=yes
	secret=(Password)
	type=peer
	username=(TelNumber)
USER Context	
USER Details	
Register String	(TelNumber):(Password)@(VoIPHost)/(TelNumber)

Index

Symbols

A

B

Z

ZapBarge 241
Zap fields
additional fields 55-57
busycount option 57
busydetect option 57
callprogress option 57

channel field 55
echocancel option 56
echotraining option 57
echowhenbridged option 56
immediate option 56
Zaptel (Zap) 45
Zaptel option 134
Zork, games 229

Thank you for buying
FreePBX 2.5
Powerful Telephony Solutions

Packt Open Source Project Royalties

When we sell a book written on an Open Source project, we pay a royalty directly to that project. Therefore by purchasing FreePBX 2.5 Powerful Telephony Solutions, Packt will have given some of the money received to the FreePBX project.

In the long term, we see ourselves and you—customers and readers of our books—as part of the Open Source ecosystem, providing sustainable revenue for the projects we publish on. Our aim at Packt is to establish publishing royalties as an essential part of the service and support a business model that sustains Open Source.

If you're working with an Open Source project that you would like us to publish on, and subsequently pay royalties to, please get in touch with us.

Writing for Packt

We welcome all inquiries from people who are interested in authoring. Book proposals should be sent to author@packtpub.com. If your book idea is still at an early stage and you would like to discuss it first before writing a formal book proposal, contact us; one of our commissioning editors will get in touch with you.

We're not just looking for published authors; if you have strong technical skills but no writing experience, our experienced editors can help you develop a writing career, or simply get some additional reward for your expertise.

About Packt Publishing

Packt, pronounced 'packed', published its first book "Mastering phpMyAdmin for Effective MySQL Management" in April 2004 and subsequently continued to specialize in publishing highly focused books on specific technologies and solutions.

Our books and publications share the experiences of your fellow IT professionals in adapting and customizing today's systems, applications, and frameworks. Our solution-based books give you the knowledge and power to customize the software and technologies you're using to get the job done. Packt books are more specific and less general than the IT books you have seen in the past. Our unique business model allows us to bring you more focused information, giving you more of what you need to know, and less of what you don't.

Packt is a modern, yet unique publishing company, which focuses on producing quality, cutting-edge books for communities of developers, administrators, and newbies alike. For more information, please visit our website: www.PacktPub.com.

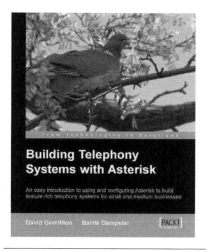

Building Telephony Systems With Asterisk

ISBN: 1-904811-15-9   Paperback: 176 pages

An easy introduction to using and configuring Asterisk to build feature-rich telephony systems for small and medium businesses

1. Install, configure, deploy, secure, and maintain Asterisk

2. Build a fully-featured telephony system and create a dial plan that suits your needs

3. Learn from example configurations for different requirements

Asterisk Gateway Interface 1.4 and 1.6 Programming

ISBN: 978-1-847194-46-6   Paperback: 220 pages

Design and develop Asterisk-based VoIP telephony platforms and services using PHP and PHPAGI

1. Develop voice-enabled applications utilizing the collective power of Asterisk, PHP, and the PHPAGI class library

2. Learn basic elements of a FastAGI server utilizing PHP and PHPAGI

3. Develop new Voice 2.0 mash ups using the Asterisk Manager

4. Add Asterisk application development skills to your development arsenal, enriching your market offering and experience

Please check **www.PacktPub.com** for information on our titles

Printed in Great Britain by
Amazon.co.uk, Ltd.,
Marston Gate.